WHY YOU WON'T GO TO HEAVEN
THOUGH A MURDERER MIGHT!

by
STEPHEN

100th Century Publishing
5110 Lincoln Ave.
Evansville, IN 47715

Published by 100th Century
New York * London * Toronto * Sidney * Tokyo * Amsterdam
(just kidding — we haven't actually opened these offices yet)

100th Century Publishing
5110 Lincoln Avenue
Evansville IN 47715

WHY YOU WON'T GO TO HEAVEN
Though a Murderer Might!

First Printing, 1994

10 9 8 7 6 5 4 3 2 1

Copyright ©1994 by Stephen Richard Schwambach

Cover illustration by Bill Graf

Back cover photograph by Tim Bennett

Publisher's Cataloging in Publication
(Prepared by Quality Books Inc.)

Schwambach, Stephen, 1948-
Why You Won't Go To Heaven: Though A Murderer Might! / Stephen.
p. cm.
ISBN 0-9639172-7-7

1. Murder—Fiction. 2. Skating—Fiction. I. Title

PS3569.C853W49 1994   813'.54
                           QBI94-735

All rights reserved.

Without limiting the rights under copyright reserved above, no part of this publication may be reproduced, stored in or introduced into a retrieval system, or transmitted, in any form or by any means (electronic, mechanical, photocopying, recording or otherwise), without the prior written permission of both the copyright owner and the above publisher of this book.

If you purchased this book without a cover you should be aware that this book is stolen property. It was reported as "unsold and destroyed" to the publisher and neither the author nor the publisher has received any payment for this "stripped book."

Publisher's Note:
These stories are works of fiction. Names, characters, places, and incidents either are the product of the author's imagination or are used fictitiously, and any resemblance to actual persons, living or dead, events, or locales is entirely coincidental.

PRINTED IN THE UNITED STATES OF AMERICA

To my friend and partner, Bill Butterfield
Thanks for believing in me

THANKS TO ...

    Judy — you get better every year.

    Pete and Tab — you've stretched me; I'm a stronger, wiser man because of you.

    Abi, Beki, Abe and Ariel — for reminding me of what is really important in life.

    Dad — some people are all talk and no action; you're just the opposite.

    Kent — nobody has edited me better. You improved the manuscript a full grade level. Maybe two.

    Carol — you were right. Sometimes silver is better than gold.

    Mike — for caring so deeply about my deadlines when you had deadlines of your own.

    Tony — for teaching me what a servant's heart is all about.

    Beth — you're good and you're great to work with, cousin.

    Judy Haywood — for giving me more than I asked for and doubling the impact of the chapter.

    Dennis Buickel and Dr. John Heidingsfelder — you went the extra mile. When I left, I didn't have to guess.

    Wayne Westling — other legal experts were afraid of the controversy; you took the time to tell a stranger what he needed to know.

    Bill Graf — what a stunning painting for the cover. You moved swiftly and gave me exactly what I asked for.

    The people I serve and with whom I work — for letting this be part of what I do.

WHY YOU WON'T GO TO HEAVEN
Though a Murder Might!

The Day of Your Death 6

Chapter 1 — Why a Sincere Person Won't Go 17

Chapter 2 — Why a Good Person Won't Go 25

Chapter 3 — Why a Religious Person Won't Go 41

Chapter 4 — Why a Church Member Won't Go 55

Chapter 5 — Why a "Born-Again" Person Won't Go 67

Chapter 6 — Why a Clergyman Won't Go 79

Chapter 7 — Why a Murderer Might 93

The Day of Your Life 117

INTRODUCTION

THE DAY OF YOUR DEATH

And, live we how we can, yet die we must.
—William Shakespeare

1

No blatant warning, no spine-prickling premonition — not even an inkling.

On the contrary.

You were feeling good as you pulled onto the expressway. Traffic was light. The weather was perfect. For once, you would be home early.

You reached forward to fiddle with the radio, taking your eyes off the road for just 2.9 seconds.

But that was all it took.

The red Ford Escort that swerved across the meridian into your lane wasn't very big. But with a combined speed of both vehicles at 113 miles per hour, it didn't have to be.

Funny thing.

If you had plowed into him head-on, you may have lived. Your airbag worked perfectly.

But 2.1 seconds before impact, the man at the wheel woke with a start and slammed on his brakes. At the sound of their frantic squeal, you jerked your eyes away from the radio and caught a flash of red hurtling toward you from the left. Instinctively, you stomped the brake pedal and wrenched your steering wheel hard right.

Mistake.

Fatal mistake.

Next morning's paper described it tersely, in detached, clinical terms: "According to an unidentified motorist who stopped after witnessing the accident, 'The front bumper of the red car squarely impacted the driver's door of the second vehicle.' Both drivers were pronounced dead at the scene."

But your last 1.7 seconds of consciousness on earth were more terrifyingly eventful than that first-year reporter ever could have imagined.

Some people speculated that you never knew what hit you. But they were wrong. You could hear, you could feel, you could see. You could think.

Somehow your brain, instinctively knowing this was IT, called on every mystic, unused capacity within its power to elongate your last, precious moment of consciousness on this earth. Someone had just pushed the ultra-slow motion button of your life.

Located just one inch from your left ear, your cerebral cortex instantly registered the sound of collision as some peculiar mixture of grinding crash-thump-roar.

The entire window at your left exploded into hundreds of tiny, oddly-shaped shards of safety glass. Some of them embedded themselves in your neck and face. The rest shot through your vision in a brilliant shower of sparkling diamonds.

But it was the door frame you were counting on to protect you that was transformed into the instrument of your death.

You had the wind knocked out of you as its metal shattered your upper arm and broke every rib on the left side of your body in a straight vertical line — except for the last one, which it drove like a knife through your left lung and into your heart.

But that was only the beginning of damage wrought by your "protective" door frame. The sheer force of its impact ruptured your aorta, causing a costly tear at its weakest point just past the arch. Blood rapidly filled your left chest cavity.

Your seat belt stubbornly held you in place as the door frame, still on its lethal mission, fractured your pelvis. The sudden, powerful jolt simultaneously ripped open your bladder, mangled your liver and shredded your spleen.

Your jaw snapped in two places. Your brain slapped hard left, right, left against the bone of your skull, causing subdural hemorrhage. "No! Not ye—"

Darkness.

2

The coroner said you lived eight minutes, max, after unconsciousness. But if so, that's not how it felt to you. An instant after blackness, it seemed, you were back. But different.

You were still inside the compacted wreckage of your car. Curiously, however, you felt no pain. And you were moving...away...from your body!

A fleeting snapshot. One last, horrifying glimpse of blood-soaked flesh. The clothing yours, yes, but the rest unrecognizable. Your own mother wouldn't have...

Out. Floating slowly, smoothly upward above the accident scene, you could see the frantic movements of men trying in vain to reach the dead drivers. Shouts...cars crazily angled...traffic backed up to 2nd Avenue, horns honking...red and blue flashing lights in the distance, wailing sirens...everything becoming smaller, sounds becoming fainter, as higher and higher you rose.

Not alone. Suddenly, you are aware of unmistakable Presence on both sides. But you will not, cannot look. They are lifting...higher...faster. This couldn't — nothing like this has ever —

Warp speed blur.

Blackness.

No air. No need.

Nowhere.

No time...........

3

Somewhere.
Blackness gives way to light.
Dazzling. Awesome.
What in the — ?
Hey. You have body!
Hands, arms, legs, feet...but different, new, with new capacity, new capability. You sense this form may be only temporary, like a loaner while yours in the shop.
You slow down. The blur clears.
Something huge materializes. And you are standing before the tall gates of an unimaginably beautiful city. Your eyes widen, attempting to take it all in — the breadth, the height, the vast scale of its architecture...impossible. Even your new capacity cannot begin to grasp its essence.
The building codes must be different, here. What an absurd thought. Earth's construction rules no longer apply. How could they? Something more than simple gravity is here at work. How does that huge city — whatever it is — how does it suspend there at that...angle, but perfectly balanced? You are going to have to see this up close. You must, in fact.
But you're on the outside. You can see in, at least a little way. But there is so much more. The city pulsates with the glowing radiance of every precious stone known to man...and perhaps a few that man has never known. There is a pull, something like a powerful attraction that makes you really, really want to go in.
But how? You can move...you can walk...yes! You can run! And you do. But try as you might, you cannot seem to close the distance.

So you slow to a stop.
And wait.
And wait.

4

All at once you are overwhelmed by the presence of Radiant Majesty. Your knees buckle as before the brilliance of the sun, and you fall prostrate at His feet.

For you know not how long, silence. You try to catch your breath, but you have none.

And then it comes — in a Voice that surrounds and sweeps over you like rushing waters — the inevitable, haunting, central question of your existence...one question only, the only question, the only question...

"Why should I allow you to enter?"

The Voice echoes in your mind as you try to gather your wits. Think. Must think.

He...He wants to know why He should allow me to enter —

Heaven!

This is Heaven!

You always knew — well, that is, you always thought there must be a — no wonder your entire being yearns to go inside, to experience its...

Oh, God.

If there's a heaven, then there must be a...

No. Don't even think it.

All you have to do is answer the question. That's all. Answer the question, answer the question. Nothing to worry about if you can just answer the question.

It's not as though you hadn't thought about this before — eons ago, it seems, but you had! You...you had a philosophy...a logical, quite reasonable...yes!

That's it!

Giddy with relief, you open your mouth to respond, when terror freezes the answer midway in your throat. Your mind goes numb at the total inadequacy of the flippant solution you had arrived at on earth. You dare not, will not — cannot! — mumble the inanity that was supposed to have been your reply. You are absolutely speechless.

And in that instant, you know you are damned.

The awful finality of that reality crashes in on you. Bereft of all hope, stripped of all excuse, your body shakes uncontrollably.

From somewhere, you hear the sound of someone sobbing. The sound comes closer, and closer, and louder, and louder, until you realize — the sound is you.

This.
This is what it was all about. This is the only thing that mattered. Everything depended on this...and you — you weren't even close. One life. One chance. One shot at all eternity.

And you blew it.

5

For billions of us — in fact, for the majority of the human race — such a scenario goes beyond mere speculation.

It is prophecy.

It is shame. It is all the nightmares you ever had, rolled up into one and infinitely surpassed. It is sickening, gut-wrenching tragedy.

And it is fact: as things now stand, you almost certainly will not go to heaven. Without fear of the slightest exaggeration, you may call that frightening prospect...pure hell.

Would you like to know why you won't go to heaven?

With all my heart, I wish I knew how to tell you. But even if I knew, no matter how true the words I would speak, I know you wouldn't listen. Not here. Not now. Not this way.

And frankly, I don't blame you. It would be too much to believe, wouldn't it? It would be too much for you to suppose that a mere mortal could not only decipher his own eternal destiny, but that he could also somehow have discovered where you, too, will spend eternity. And Why.

How unbearably sad. For if you knew why you won't go to heaven, then perhaps...just perhaps...you might be able to alter your destiny.

What a wretched dilemma! Deep within the very core of your being, you ache with a desperate, even frantic, need to know. But your intellect will never permit me to come boldly forward and give you the facts.

Even if I had them.

And I'm not saying that I do.

Your stubborn pride would immediately reject the utter simplicity of what I would attempt to share.

No.

No, if there is any hope for you at all, you will have to discover the startling truth for yourself.

Now, that — that I might be able to help you with.

Or not.

6

Question: What if the Answer were already inside you, included as standard equipment so that no one who really wanted to go to heaven would be left without a map?
I'm just asking.

Have you ever had a name on the tip of your tongue, but try though you might, you couldn't remember it? Frustrating, isn't it? But if only someone would give you one good clue — well, maybe two or three — you just know you could remember it instantly.

So...what if your Creator dropped a few of His clues about...sprinkled them, as it were, throughout the events of our everyday lives? In fact, what if He secreted His triggering clues in the very heart of those incidents, large and small, that make up the whole of our lives?

If He's a loving God, and if He really wants to spend forever with the people who really want to spend forever with Him, that's not so far-fetched.

Is it?

But if so, there's a challenge built in. Just enough of one to filter out the people who aren't really interested.

Our problem is that we're too close to all the clues. Typically, what we see everywhere is ignored. In a familiar room we no longer see the wallpaper — the pattern of which we couldn't describe if our lives depended on it. It's like the constant gurgling of the filter in an aquarium that our brains no longer permit our ears to hear.

Most of us are like that. We have eyes, but we no longer see. We have ears, but we no longer hear.

Until somebody mentions wallpaper while we're in that familiar room. Until someone near the aquarium says, "What's that sound?"

Would you let me do that for you?

7

I am about to tell you seven stories. They are pure fiction, which means that they are true.

And if they are true, then what you are about to see and hear are seven clues. Seven clues that may allow you to discover why you won't go to heaven.

Unless you have lost all sensitivity — unfortunately, a condition that is not especially rare — what you are about to read can set Truth vibrating inside you like a tuning fork that leaps to life when it hears its sympathetic note.

The first six clues can help you discover deep within your psyche the awful truth about why you won't go to heaven.

If your longing is great enough, at some unpredictable point while you are pondering these six clues, the light will suddenly dawn.

And then you will know.

When that happens, you will be torn apart by two powerful emotions. On the one hand, you will experience the excitement of having discovered the hidden compartment that has always been inside you. The implications of that find are enormous, for there is only One who could have secreted it there. To know that you now know the unknowable...will leave you tingling with awe.

On the other hand, you will be forced to grapple with the stark reality that the truth you have just discovered pronounces your own sentence of death.

It is then — and only then — that you will be ready to approach the final clue with any hope of unlocking its mystery. Until you arrive at the awareness of your own inescapable plight, you can read the seventh story a hundred times and still come up empty. But once the utter finality of your own hopelessness has fully sunk in, you will have at last arrived at the vantage point from which you can explore the unthinkable: how it is that though you, a fairly normal, basically decent person, won't go to heaven...

a murderer might.

8

Many readers will be unwilling or unable to grasp this final, infuriating, wonderful truth. In their case, I am so sorry. Please forgive me. I genuinely wish there was something more I could do.

But if somehow you make it all the way to the end of the seventh clue without surrendering to exasperated rejection...if somehow in a moment or a month this startling revelation suddenly bursts forth from within you in shocking, crystal clarity...then for you there will still be hope.

It is in that hope that I now tell you these seven stories.

Somewhere in each of them is hidden a shard of truth, buried deeply in plain sight. If as you read you think you have found one of them, handle it gently, being careful not to break off any of its oddly-shaped protrusions. You don't want any gaps when, at the end, you attempt to fit them all together.

9

Oh. Before we begin, let me issue one last warning. The rare quarry you are about to so diligently pursue is deceptively simple. Maddeningly so. Keep in mind that only lies are complicated. By contrast, Truth is pure and equally accessible to both the intellectual and to the mentally impoverished.

It is ironic. But all too often the fast are slow to arrive, while the slow are able to grasp its essence almost instantly. Once comprehended, however, its profundity will challenge the most brilliant mind.

Then it will tax it. After that, it will overwhelm it.

And then that mind will be given the chance to do the Thing it never imagined it would desire...
...or Be Desired...
...to do.

WHY A SINCERE PERSON WON'T GO

*Forgive his crimes, forgive his virtues too,
Those smaller faults, half converts to the right.*

—Ralph Waldo Emerson

1

She pushed the down button of the elevator.

"Jessica!" Kevin called and waved at her from the door of his office. "Give me one minute, and I'll walk you to your car!"

Jessica opened her mouth to decline the invitation, but he had already ducked back inside for his coat. Oh, well, she was in no hurry tonight. And it was rather nice of him to offer.

He would ask her out again, of course, and once again she would have to say no. Even after five months, it was still too soon.

"Thanks for waiting." Kevin bustled toward her with a wide grin on his face, briefcase in one hand. He fumbled to fasten the top button of his overcoat with his other hand.

"Thanks for offering to walk with me," she smiled. "But you may change your mind when I tell you where I'm parked."

"Outside the garage, huh?" said Kevin. "I thought as much when I saw you come in late this morning."

"And that was all I needed! First, Carrie was too sick to go to school, so I had to find a sitter. Then with all the snow last night, traffic was slowed to a crawl."

The elevator door opened. It was jammed with people, and they rode down in silence. As they jostled against each other in the main floor lobby, Kevin asked, "So where are you parked?"

"In the lot across the street from Nottingham's."

"Nottingham's? That's a five-block walk."

"Tell me about it. The sidewalks this morning were a sheet of ice."

"So take my arm," he said, as they left the building. "If I start to fall you can catch me."

"Ha! In these high heels? I'd fall on top of you!"

"I wouldn't mind."

She glanced at him. He stopped grinning.

"Sorry about the crack." They walked half a block before Kevin spoke again. "Look, why don't you let me make it up to you with dinner tonight? Anywhere you like. I promise I'll be the perfect gentleman."

"Not tonight. I really do need to nurse my sick daughter."

"How about Friday? She'll be okay by then, won't she?"

"She may be, but I won't."

"Whew!" Kevin whistled. "I think I've just been put in my place."

They walked another half-block before she attempted to explain. "This isn't about you, Kevin. It's about me. I guess I don't heal as quickly as some people. You seemed to get over your divorce even before it was final."

"Hey, low blow!"

"I'm sorry. Perhaps I'm envious." She changed the subject. "So what project are you working on now?"

Kevin's answer lasted the rest of the way to the parking lot, and she relaxed.

2

They stopped beside her car, Jessica angling her purse under one of the lot's buzzing lights to fish for her keys.

Kevin waited until she found them. "How much more time do you need?"

Back to that, again. She looked up at him. "Why do you have to know?"

"Because I intend to keep asking you out until you say yes."

"Why me? There must be a hundred other women in the building who have gotten over their divorces quite nicely."

"Maybe they're not my type."

"Maybe I'm not, either."

Kevin tilted his head back and exhaled a cloud of steam into the night air. "Maybe you're not. But I wish you'd give us both the chance to find out."

Jessica snapped her purse shut. "What are you looking for, Kevin? A wife? A friend? A lover?"

"Hey, I just —"

"Because I'll tell you what I'm looking for. I'm looking for a whole lot more. I want some answers. And they're not the sort of answers I'll get in some man's bedroom."

"Look, I didn't say anything about —"

"No, you didn't. But you didn't have to. If I had wanted you to take me to bed tonight, you would have been only too happy to oblige me. And that bothers me. It bothers me a lot."

"I'm a man, Jessica."

"And I'm a woman. So what? You think I don't miss it? If Darin and I had anything, we had that. But it wasn't enough." She looked away. "Not nearly enough."

"You had a bad experience, that's all."

"Sex wasn't enough, money wasn't enough, Carrie wasn't enough..."

"So, he was a jerk."

"No, he wasn't!"

Kevin backed up one step. He searched her face. "You're still in love with him."

"No, I'm not. Not the way you think. Darin and I didn't split up because he's a jerk. For that matter, you didn't leave your wife because she was a jerk. Nobody who —"

"She left me. And she was a jerk."

"So maybe we're all jerks, Kevin — you, me, Darin, your wife — maybe everybody in the whole wide world is a jerk!"

"Thank you very much."

Jessica closed her eyes and sighed. "Why do you keep trying to make this personal?"

"I take being called a jerk personally, that's why. Hey, the last thing on my mind tonight was arguing with a pretty lady on a downtown parking lot in fifteen-degree weather. My teeth are starting to chatter!"

"I can handle the cold outside," said Jessica. "It's the cold inside I can't handle."

Kevin touched her shoulder. "You're lonely, Jessica. You've got to go out and live a little. Look, in spite of what you think, all I wanted tonight was a date. I thought maybe we could —"

"And that's why I just don't have the heart for it, Kevin. All you want tonight is a date."

"So what else is there?"

Jessica's eyes flashed, but he cut her off before she could reply. "No, I mean it! Some good food, a glass of wine to take the chill off. Some good times."

"The good times never last, Kevin."

"So enjoy them while they do."

"That's it? That's your philosophy of life — go from good time to good time? What about all the times in between?"

"You...you look forward to the next good time!"

"And how long do you propose to keep this up, Kevin?"

"How long — good grief! My whole life, I guess."

"Uh-huh, and after that?"

"After what?"

"After your last good time, then what?"

"Then you die."

"And after you die, what?"

"I dunno. Go to heaven, I guess."

"Go to heaven, you guess."

"Sure, why not?"

"And what makes you think you'll get in?"

Kevin grinned. "Because I'm not a jerk!"

"Kevin, I'm serious."

"Hey, so am I! I'm not a jerk! I don't pretend to be somebody I'm not. With me, what you see is what you get. I mean, as far as I'm concerned, the Man Upstairs...he doesn't care. Just as long as you're sincere — you know what I mean."

"Just as long as you're sincere?"

"Sure. Say, how did we get on religion? That's not exactly —"

"So what if you're sincerely wrong?"

Kevin blinked, then shook his head. "I think I've lost you."

"Yes, you have."

They stood facing each other then, not speaking, their hands and feet starting to go numb in the cold.

Kevin broke the silence. "I don't know about you,

but I'm frozen. What do you say we call a truce and continue this another time — someplace where it's warm?"

Jessica smiled. "I'm sorry. Thank you for walking me to my car. Be careful that you don't slip and break your neck on the way back."

"Spoken like a mother. Tell Carrie for me that she's lucky to have you."

"Thank you. And Kevin — as jerks go, you're a very nice jerk."

He laughed and walked away.

3

Still clutching her keys in her shaking hand, Jessica turned to open her car door, praying the lock wasn't frozen. It wasn't. Thank God, she thought and grimaced as she slid in on the cold seat.

Now, if only it would start. Her car was used to the shelter of the parking garage, not an exposed lot.

The first slow grinding sound of the ignition caused her to panic. Get hold of yourself, she thought. Press the accelerator all the way to the floor...ease it back out...there. Now, try again.

Nothing.

She should have asked Kevin to stay until she got the car started. Frantically, she wiped a hole in the haze on her windshield to see if Kevin was still in sight.

There he was, just getting ready to cross the street.

She saw Kevin dutifully wait for the light to change, then step off the curb, head down, shoulders hunched against the cold.

At that same moment, in a black blur from his left, she saw the skidding garbage truck. It slammed, swallowed, and ejected Kevin's body in the middle of the intersection.

No!

Jessica tore her eyes away from the grisly sight to a flurry of movement sixty feet past, where the truck driver fought the truck to a stop, threw open his door and half-fell out of the cab. She saw him jam a fist to his mouth and sag against the side of his truck.

Shaking uncontrollably, Jessica slowly forced her horrified gaze to return to the mangled form in the middle of the street.

Kevin's body was absolutely still.

The hot breath of Jessica's scream billowed against her window, obliterating the image from her sight.

WHY A GOOD PERSON WON'T GO

The greatest difficulties lie where we are not looking for them.

—Goethe

1

Addom Mitchell fanned through the pages of a magazine in the waiting room outside his boss' office. It was a bad idea to buck Trafford this soon, but he had no other choice.

Barely eight months ago, Credit General had swallowed up the smaller CMT Credit Services in a lightening-swift move. Nearly all of CMT's middle managers, including Addom, had been caught by surprise. Like most of his peers, Addom had been relieved to learn he would keep his job.

Three months later, however, he had a new boss. Baker Trafford blew into town with a briefcase full of big city ideas and a steely get-with-the-program-or-you're-history intention to implement every one of them.

"We've got too many big-shots around here," he announced in his first managers' meeting. "You're out of touch. You have no idea what's happening in the real world, out on the street.

"Managers who live in ivory towers make bad decisions. So starting next week all managers will spend one full day out of every month working — and I mean working! — at an entry-level position. You'll report to a different place in the company each month, and I'll make the assignments. Oh. One other thing. For that day, you will be paid the wage scale that goes with the job. Any questions?"

Unlike some of the other managers who used the weekend to update their resumes, Addom admired the man's bold move. It had gained Trafford instant popularity with the rest of the work force. It also quickly weeded out most of the uncooperative managers, reducing the number of people Trafford would have to fire. A year from now, Trafford would be firmly in charge of a leaner, service-oriented company that functioned as a team.

All in all, it was a shrewdly calculated way to come in and shake things up. So. While others looked for new jobs or wasted time treading water, Addom seized the opportunity to move up.

On Monday he reported to buildings and grounds, where he spent eight hours cutting grass, changing light bulbs — and impressing people with the good-natured way he took the inevitable ribbing. The following month he joined the secretarial pool, where his computer-sharpened typing skills enabled him to function quite nicely. He even had fun getting coffee for his female boss — something the other secretaries had stopped doing long ago.

But this month was different. He tossed his unread magazine back on the table and checked his watch. Brother, was this month's assignment different! Less than sixty seconds after receiving the memo, he had picked up the phone and asked for this meeting with Trafford.

Next Monday he was scheduled to spend the entire day making house calls on delinquent accounts. There was no way. As far as he was concerned, this was the worst part of the business he was in. This ate at him the most — in his company's pursuit of profit, it often loaned money to people who had no business borrowing.

Inevitably, a depressing percentage of these people suffered a financial setback through ignorance or incompetence. And then this big, friendly company that was only too eager to loan them the money a few months ago would suddenly turn mean. His company's ruthless system started with threatening letters, then moved to rude phone calls, and finally sent collection agents to these poor people's homes.

Addom had heard the stories about little old widows hiding behind the couches in their living rooms, afraid to go to the door. He wasn't about to become one of the goons they had to hide from. This was where he drew the line. He would simply explain that —

"Excuse me, Mr. Mitchell. Mr. Trafford will see you now."

2

This was the third time Addom had been in his new boss' office. Gone were the expensive oil paintings, indirect lighting and plush draperies of his predecessor. Newly-installed fluorescent tubes exposed every square inch of the large room to bright work light. The walls were covered with constantly-updated charts that tracked the most critical functions of Credit General's operations. Naked windows opened to a view that some insisted Trafford had yet to see.

"Sit down, Mitchell," said Trafford, who was signing the last of a sheaf of papers. "You're here to try to beg out of your assignment this month." He looked up, then, just in time to read the surprised expression on Addom's face.

"Tell me I'm wrong," said Trafford.

"You're...not wrong," Addom admitted, as he lowered himself into the armless chair at the edge of Trafford's desk. "How did you —"

"How did I know you would balk at collections? Mitchell, you're as easy to see through as a rookie salesman's expense report. You took this job, what was it, five years ago —?"

"Six."

"—six years ago, because you liked the prestige of working for a financial institution. Money. You like making it, you like working around it, you like managing it. But in six long years, you have yet to come to grips with where all this money comes from."

"With all due respect, Sir, I know where our money comes from. Our loan rates are too high for the average person to give us a second thought. We make our profit loaning money to people who can't afford to borrow it. And then, when they can't keep up with their payments, we go after them without any pity whatsoever."

Trafford stood up and walked over to the window. During the silence that followed Addom's speech, he gazed out at the view he wasn't supposed to know existed.

Trafford said quietly, "You're not the first person to say that about this company, Mitchell." Trafford smoothed a hand across the top of his thinning hair. "It's interesting, isn't it? As long as you didn't have to face these 'poor' people you feel so sorry for, you managed to live with your powerful conscience just fine.

"Their money spent just fine, when you bought your first new car, when you made that down payment on your house, when you paid for your Hawaii vacation. But I find it instructive to note when you suddenly got religion."

Trafford turned his head from the window and looked over his left shoulder at Mitchell. "It was when somebody told you that you were going to have to go out and do the dirty work yourself."

Addom held Trafford's gaze and thought, he's about to fire me.

Trafford left the window and returned to his chair. "You say we're taking advantage of these people. I say we're giving them a leg up! Sure, we have to charge them more interest — their default rate is higher and that makes the cost of doing business with them greater. But we give people with no credit their first chance. We give people with lousy credit a second, third and fourth chance.

"Do a lot of them fall on their faces? Absolutely. But a whole lot more of them make it. Those are the ones we never see again. Because the next time they want to buy a car, they go across the street to apply for the cheaper rate of our competitor. And guess what? Thanks to the brand new credit rating they've earned with us, good old Conservative National gives it to them."

Still seated, Trafford leaned across his desk toward Addom. "Do you know what we do around here, Mitchell? We give a chance to the people nobody else believes in!

"The ones who blow their chance, we go after. Because if we didn't, we'd have to eat the loss and charge the people who pay on time an even higher rate of interest. Is that what you'd recommend we do?"

Addom had never seen this side of Trafford. He doubted if anyone else in the company had, either. "I

— I don't know what to think. You've made some good points, but —"

"Well, let me make one more," Trafford interrupted. "Come Monday morning, you're going to be knocking on deadbeats' doors, so we can afford to keep ours open. Or you can walk straight out of this office and go empty your desk."

For a moment, neither man moved. Then Addom slowly rose from his chair and walked toward the door.

"Mitchell!"

One hand on the doorknob, Addom turned to look at his boss.

"I like you. That's why I gave you this assignment. You lick this, and there's no limit to how far you can go in this company."

Trafford turned his attention to a thick report on his desk. "That's all."

3

On Monday morning Addom bent over a city map in the front seat of his car, still employed by Credit General. "Canal Street. Canal...Canal...there it is. Now, 2710...turn left, I guess. Okay. Here goes."

If someone had asked him why he had stayed, he would have probably replied, "I don't know."

Certainly, he was loathe to admit there was one part of his job that he couldn't do. Refusing assignments had never been his style. He had built a career out of his image as a can-do guy.

Perhaps part of it was his respect for Trafford. There was no denying that the man intrigued him. Working for him was exciting. It was like being committed to a cause.

"Do you know what we do around here, Mitchell? We give a chance to the people nobody else believes

in!"
 That was quite a line. Addom wondered if Trafford believed it.

4

 By 3:00 p.m. Addom was starting to feel a little better. Until today, he hadn't understood how Credit General could afford to employ full-time collection agents to make house calls. Now he understood. There was nothing like showing up at someone's front door and telling them you had come for payment. No matter how many other companies they owed, meeting their creditor face-to-face forced customers to suddenly make Credit General their number one bill-paying priority. So far, he had collected $3,200 from people who wrote him checks on the spot. He smiled. Whether or not their checks were good was someone else's worry.
 And he hadn't encountered the kind of rude resistance he had expected. Some of them even apologized for causing him to make a special trip. Only two of his calls had been to belligerents, one of whom ordered him off his property. After enduring their verbal abuse, Addom would lose no sleep over recommending legal proceedings against both of them.
 And then he rang the doorbell at 1707 Sweetser Avenue.

5

 A plump, stooped little woman opened the door halfway and cautiously peered out at him.
 "Yes?"
 "Are you Mrs. Rudensky?"

"Yes, I am," she replied fearfully, it seemed to Addom. Her round, wrinkled face reminded him of his own grandmother.

"Mrs. Rudensky, I'm Addom Mitchell, with Credit General." I'm here to collect the —"

"What did you say?"

Oh, great, Addom thought. She's hard-of-hearing. He raised his voice, hoping none of her neighbors could hear. He didn't want to embarrass her. "I said my name is Addom Mitchell. I'm with Credit General."

"Credit General?" she said and lifted her hand to her wobbly chin. "I don't believe I —"

This wasn't working. "Mrs. Rudensky, may I please come inside? Just for a minute. So we can talk privately?"

Addom's request made the old woman tremble. With one hand balancing her trifocals on her nose, she looked Addom up and down, taking in his dark burgundy wing-tips, his conservative suit and tie underneath the beige raincoat, his closely-cropped hair, his serious, nice-looking face. Addom smiled.

"Well...I suppose it'll be all right," she decided. She opened the door wider.

As Addom followed the shuffling woman into her living room, he shook his head at the vulnerability of older people. She should never have let him in. The next man who showed up at her door wearing a suit might hit her in the head and steal everything she had.

"Please have a seat," she gestured toward the sofa. "May I fix you something to drink?"

"No, no thank you," said Addom. "I just need a moment of your time."

He waited as Mrs. Rudensky eased herself into the chair across from him. "Do you like this living room suit?" she asked, just as Addom was about to speak.

"Oh. Yes, it's very nice," Addom replied. He glanced at the brightly-colored sofa, love seat, and chairs. They seemed out of place, amidst all the other older furniture.

"Albert picked this out and had it delivered last June, right before he died. He did it without my knowing. A surprise for our sixtieth wedding anniversary."

Her quavering voice reminded him of his grandmother, too. So did the way she leaned forward, holding on to the right arm of the overstuffed chair. He guessed old people who lived alone did that because there was no one to help them up if they sank too far back.

"That was a very thoughtful anniversary gift," said Addom. "Mrs. Rudensky, the reason I'm —"

"I was so angry with him!" Mrs. Rudensky continued, oblivious to Addom's attempt to avoid personalities and get down to business. "He said our old sofa and chairs were worn clear through, so he had them hauled away. Well, they were in sad shape, it's true, but they were so full of memories, from the time when all the children were growing up. Besides, we didn't need to spend all that money, and I told him so. But he wouldn't listen."

Addom squirmed on the new couch. He had an idea where Mr. Rudensky had found the money for the new living room suit.

"At first I wouldn't even sit on it. Albert would say, 'Come, sit down on the new chair I bought for you!'

"And I would say, 'It's not comfortable. I like this old one, better.'

"But then, Albert took sick, and I practically lived at the hospital until his death. It was all such an exhausting blur, such a horrible nightmare..."

She fell silent. Addom noticed the loud "tick-tock" coming from an ancient clock on the mantle above Mrs. Rudensky's head. Now was his chance to tell her his reason for being there. But he couldn't.

Mrs. Rudensky let out a big sigh and resumed her story before Addom could take advantage of the opening. "When I came back to the house that evening after the funeral, the first thing I noticed was this living room suit that I had so hated. But all at once, it dawned on me that this was the last thing my husband had given me before he died. I went right over to this chair, sat down in it, and I've been sitting in it every day, ever since."

His worst fears had come true! He wanted to slither out of this poor old woman's house on his belly, like the snake that he was. He had to get a grip on himself, do his job, and get out.

"Uh, Mrs. Rudensky, do you know how your husband, uh, arranged to pay for this furniture?"

"No, no. Albert always took care of the finances — out of our savings, I guess. But I'm not mad about that anymore."

Addom groped for words. He had to come up with a gentle way to break the news to her. "Mrs. Rudensky, is it possible that your husband borrowed the money?"

"Borrowed?" Her heavily-creased brow furrowed. "I don't see why...Albert would never do anything like that. There was no need."

Great. He tried another tack. "What about all the correspondence from my company, Mrs. Rudensky? You know, the letters? The bills?"

"What's that? Bills? I don't get many. Ethel — she's my next-door neighbor. She's a widow woman, too — she helps me pay my water bill, my gas, my electric...."

"Mrs. Rudensky, what about all the letters you received from Credit General? Why haven't you responded to them?"

"Credit General? No...that doesn't ring a bell. Ethel always tells me to just throw away the junk mail. People are forever trying to sell you something you don't need."

Please. This isn't happening, thought Addom. "But we called you, Mrs. Rudensky. My company — Credit General — called you on the telephone a number of times."

"Oh, the telephone. Yes, sometimes I get calls, mostly from more people wanting to sell me things. I don't hear as well as I used to. When I can't make out what they're saying, or when they don't make sense, Ethel says I should just hang up."

I've got to wind this up, fast, Addom told himself. "Mrs. Rudensky, you mentioned something about savings, a moment ago. Is it possible that you could...what I mean, is, if I — if someone — presented you with a large bill...if a major expense should come up...I take it you would have the money to cover it. From your savings, that is."

"Oh, yes!" Mrs. Rudensky smiled, nodding. "Albert always said not to worry. He took care of everything."

Addom sighed. He was going to survive this, after all.

"But you know, I am having such a problem with our bank. I've called them three times, now, to find out how much is in our savings. They say they have no such account, just the checking! Well, I tell them there must be some mistake, because my Albert took care of everything. Then they tell me they'll check into it and have someone call. But they never do."

"Another bank —" blurted Addom. "— is it possible your husband had his savings with another bank?"

"Oh, no," the old woman shook her head firmly. "He knew the people at our bank. He said they were the only bank in town he could trust."

Mrs. Rudensky leaned toward Addom and lowered her voice. "But, I'm not so sure about that any more. They must have hired some new people, because they keep making mistakes with my affairs. Ethel says they've started returning my checks, marked, 'Insufficient funds!' Can you imagine?"

Addom could. In fact, he could imagine lots of things. He could imagine that Albert hadn't exactly been the financial genius his wife imagined him to be. He could imagine that Mrs. Rudensky had probably spent the last dollar that remained in their checking account. He could imagine that the bank was not ever going to call and report to Mrs. Rudensky that they had finally located her misplaced savings.

Further, he could imagine that very soon, four almost-new pieces of furniture were going to be missing from this poor old woman's living room. And it was no trouble at all for him to imagine that, with Ethel as her financial advisor, in less than a year, Mrs. Rudensky would lose her home. What would she think of her dear, departed Albert then?

Wait a minute. Her family. "You mentioned that you had children, Mrs. Rudensky?"

"What's that?"

Addom raised his voice again. "I was asking about your family — you said something earlier about children?"

"Yes, yes, two girls and a boy. Looking back, Albert and I always said those were the happiest days of our lives. It was, until...I lost both my girls on the same night, you know. It was a terrible automobile accident. They were with a group of their friends, having such a nice time, when..."

Mrs. Rudensky pulled a tissue from her dress pocket and dabbed at her eyes. "Belinda was nineteen, Anna was seventeen. When they told me that both of them had been killed, I nearly died, too."

What had he walked into? Here he was, invading some lonely old woman's privacy, making her cry, and all for what? To collect one lousy bill? Addom couldn't take much more of this. He had to get out.

"Is your son still living?" He had almost been afraid to ask.

"Oh, yes. Robert is my youngest. If I hadn't had him when I lost my girls, I don't know what I would have done."

Finally, thought Addom. "Does your son — Robert — live nearby, then?"

"No," said Mrs. Rudensky slowly, "although, at one time he lived in Florida."

Addom's heart sank. "He lived in Florida at one time. Are you saying...you don't know where your son lives, now?"

"He and his father didn't get along all that well. Robert was always trying out new ideas, starting new businesses. He borrowed a lot of money from us, but never paid it back — although he intended to! Albert started calling him a...well, they exchanged words the last time Robert came to visit, and after that, we lost touch."

It was absolutely none of his business, but Addom asked, anyway. "How long has it been since you've heard from your son, Mrs. Rudensky?"

The old woman bowed her head. "Eleven years."

That did it. This dear old lady's entire life had been full of tragedy, now her finances were in disarray, and Credit General had sent him to finish her off. Well, this time they had sent the wrong man.

Addom felt closed in. He needed air. He stood up. "I'd better be going."

"So soon?" said the old woman. "But you haven't said —"

"There's been a mistake. I — I shouldn't have come. I'm terribly sorry to have bothered you, Mrs. Rudensky."

She struggled to push herself up from the chair, but Addom said, "Please, don't get up. You just, just stay right there. I'll show myself out. That's where you...that's right where you belong."

6

Addom sat in his car and made no move to start the engine. It wouldn't matter what he put on his report. They would just send someone else, a professional, next time — a hard-nosed, cold-hearted professional. The next guy would send a crew to come get her furniture. In less than ten minutes they would gut her living room and deprive this old woman of her last gift from her dead husband.

It wasn't fair! If only she had someone who would give her the money for the furniture, help get her affairs in proper order, protect her, fight for her!

Addom knew a man who had the ability to do all of that. In fact, that man was sitting in his car outside the old woman's house at this very moment.

The trouble was, Addom didn't know if this man had the guts to move from spectator to player. Up to this point in his life, the man Addom knew had cared enough to feel bad about injustice, but had never been willing to inconvenience himself so much as to do one blessed thing about it.

What time was it?

Addom glanced at his watch. Five after. Quitting time. Time to drive back to his office with all the loot he had collected and turn the old lady in. Or...time to violate every financial officer's cardinal rule and get involved. It was time to put up or shut up.

Addom's hand had just been called.

7

Addom slowly got out of his car. The "chunk" of his car door closing behind him made it official.

He had crossed the line.

As Addom reapproached the old woman's door,

his pace picked up. He was aware of a clean feeling, as though he had just stepped from the shower. He felt lighter inside. For the first time in his life he actually felt...virtuous.

Addom reached for the doorbell. He could clearly hear the old woman's loud voice, carrying through the door from her living room.

"...and all the time he just sat there with this hang-dog look on his face. I really had him going!"

Addom stood stock-still.

"What? You'll have to speak up, Ethel...No, I didn't give him any money. Are you kidding? I didn't have to!

"Listen! Do you know what I told him? I told him the living room furniture was my last gift from my dead husband! What? Of course I divorced the old buzzard — but that wimpy bill collector hadn't done his homework! Huh? Oh, I know it! It was a scream! You should have been here!" She laughed.

Addom trembled.

"Well, I'd better finish packing. What time does our flight leave? Oh my, I've got to hang up, if we're going to make it! On the way to Atlantic City, remind me to tell you the part I made up about my girls dying on the same night in an automobile accident. The poor boy's face turned so white, I thought he was going to pass out on the floor!"

8

Addom let his hand fall away from the doorbell. He squared his shoulders, turned, and walked slowly back to his car. He stood in the street facing his car door, but did not reach into his pocket for his keys.

His right arm tightened. He clenched his right fist.

Suddenly, Addom lifted his arm high and slammed his fist down on the roof of his car with all his might.

The sound of an anguished male cry reached Addom's ears as it echoed through the empty streets of the sleepy neighborhood.

Addom didn't recognize the cry. He didn't know whether or not it belonged to him.

Nor did he care.

WHY A RELIGIOUS PERSON WON'T GO

*I come to you as a grown child
Who has had a pig-headed father*

—Ezra Pound

1

Faleesha watched the receptionist leave her counter and walk over to a door with the word, "PRIVATE" stenciled across the frosted glass. The receptionist tapped twice, then turned and smiled at Faleesha, who was seated on the opposite side of the tiny waiting room.

In a moment, a woman who looked to be about fifty years old opened the door. A pair of dark-rimmed eyeglasses hung from a gold chain around her neck. The thin-striped brown and tan business suit she wore accented her trim figure.

"Ms. Knowlton," said the receptionist, "there's someone here to see you. She has some questions she'd like to ask."

Startled, Faleesha stood up. "No! I...I just wanted to take home some of your materials, that's all. I don't think I'm ready to —"

"Now, don't be shy," said the receptionist. "Ms. Knowlton won't bite. You'll like her. Go on in!"

Faleesha ventured a nervous glance toward the door that led outside.

Ms. Knowlton quickly walked over and extended her hand. "My name is Colin Knowlton," she said. Her voice was low and pleasant. "May I ask yours?"

Faleesha looked at her hand but didn't take it. "Faleesha," she said, finally.

"What a lovely name," Ms. Knowlton smiled. "Faleesha...?"

"Johnson."

"Faleesha Johnson," said Ms. Knowlton. "Do you mind if I ask how old you are, Faleesha?"

Faleesha's eyes darted left, right. "Eighteen," she lied.

"Well, Faleesha, thank you for coming in. Now, tell me, what can we do for you?"

Faleesha stared down at the mauve carpet. "I wanted to see if you had brochures, or something — that's all."

"Why, certainly!" said Ms. Knowlton, still smiling. "They're in my office. Why don't you come with me, and we'll see what we can find." The older woman turned and reentered her office, leaving the door open.

"Go on," smiled the receptionist, motioning her to follow.

2

Seated behind her desk, Ms. Knowlton put on her glasses and peered into the left-hand bottom drawer. "Now, let's see...so many! Here's one called, 'You and Your Body.' Here's another — 'The New Feminism.'

She looked up at Faleesha, who was perched on the edge of the ornate, cushioned chair beside her desk. "No? Don't worry, there are plenty more. Here's a favorite of a number of our clients: 'Your Life/Your Rights.' Still no? Ah, let's see...here's one called, 'I'm Pregnant — What Are My Options?' another —"

"That one," said Faleesha. "The last one you said."

"So," Ms. Knowlton smiled. She removed her glasses and leaned back in her executive swivel chair. "You're pregnant."

"I'm just late," said Faleesha. "May I have the brochure, please?" She reached for it.

"Faleesha, forgive me," said Ms. Knowlton, a look of concern on her face. "I'm not trying to be nosey...but how 'late' are you?"

Faleesha looked down at her lap. "Four...five days, I'm not sure."

"I see. I take it you haven't performed a pregnancy test, yet."

Faleesha shook her head.

"We do that here, you know — at no charge," Ms. Knowlton explained. "It's one of the services we offer. Would you like to find out for sure what you're facing? You may have nothing to worry about, you know — so why not put your mind at ease? There's no obligation, either way."

Faleesha stared at the floor. Then she nodded.

3

"I'm afraid I have bad news," said the older woman, studying Faleesha's face. After a trip to the bathroom to give a urine sample followed by a short wait, Faleesha had been ushered back into Ms. Knowlton's office.

Adjusting her glasses, the director ran her eyes once more over the pink piece of paper the receptionist had brought. "There's no doubt about it, my dear. The test came back positive. You are definitely pregnant."

Faleesha's eyes grew wide, then quickly filled with tears. Dropping her purse on the hardwood floor beside the chair, she buried her face in her hands. Her body shook.

"There, there," the older woman soothed. Faleesha felt Ms. Knowlton wrap an arm around her shoulders. "It's not the end of the world, you know." Ms. Knowlton gently pulled Faleesha's arms down. "Here, take this —"

Ms. Knowlton picked up what looked like a pointed crystal paperweight from her desk and placed the heavy object in Faleesha's trembling hands.

"There," said the older woman, enfolding Faleesha's hands within her own and squeezing. "Can you feel it? The peace? The power?"

Still sniffling, Faleesha looked down at their hands, then up at Ms. Knowlton.

"It's the power of the pyramid, Honey," said the older woman. "There is nothing in the universe quite like it for helping you get in touch with your own powers of inner healing."

Ms. Knowlton knelt down in front of her, still encircling Faleesha's hands with her own. "Now, close your eyes...come on, now, Faleesha — do as I say. That's right, that's it...now let your mind go, let yourself feel the vibrations of God."

Faleesha closed her eyes briefly, then opened them. This was too much for her.

"Don't be surprised if at first your ability to perceive the All is limited," Ms. Knowlton assured her. "In time, it will come. God is everywhere — in this room, in the air, in the trees, in the ocean...in you! The crystal pyramid you now hold in your hands vibrates to the energy patterns of God. If you let it, its power will lead you toward the Light."

Faleesha frowned and pulled away. "I...I just want to go, now."

Ms. Knowlton sighed deeply and rose to her feet. She took the crystal piece from her and placed it back on the desk. She remained standing in front of Faleesha. "And where are you going to go — to tell your boyfriend?"

Faleesha shook her head. Her eyes once again filled with tears.

"What is it?" asked Ms. Knowlton, staring at her. "Do you not know who the father is?"

Faleesha buried her face in her hands again. This time she sobbed loudly.

The older woman handed Faleesha several tissues. "Take these," she said. She stood beside Faleesha for several minutes, one hand on her shoulder, until her sobbing began to subside.

"It's not a boyfriend, is it?" asked the director. "Is it?"

Faleesha managed to shake her head no.

"Oh, god," said Ms. Knowlton disgustedly. "Men are such beasts! My poor, poor child," she murmured, once again sinking to her knees. The older woman wrapped both arms around her, pulling her close.

For another minute she hugged Faleesha, rocking her gently. Ms. Knowlton pulled back several inches and looked at her. "Is it a relative?"

Faleesha's sobbing grew louder.

The older woman hugged and rocked some more. Then she tried again. "Faleesha, Honey, trust me — you have to tell somebody, now that's all there is to it. I'll tell you what — you don't have to say anything, just nod. Okay?"

The older woman stroked Faleesha's shiny, black hair. "Was it a brother?" Faleesha didn't answer. "A cousin — somebody like that?" Faleesha still wouldn't answer. "Oh, baby, it wasn't your father, was it?" Faleesha tensed.

"Ah...has your mother remarried? Is that it, Faleesha? Is it your stepfather?"

Faleesha wailed and buried her face in the older woman's bosom, Ms. Knowlton's dangling eyeglasses poking against her right cheek.

4

"Don't you worry, Honey," the director told Faleesha after she had stopped crying. "This nightmare is only an illusion. And we're going to make it go away."

Faleesha lifted her head. "You mean an abortion, don't you?"

"It's every woman's right, dear." Ms. Knowlton paused. "But it is expensive..."

"I've got the money," said Faleesha, looking down. "Vince gave it to me."

"You mean your stepfather?"

Faleesha nodded. "He's the one who sent me here, told me to take care of it."

The director leaned back and smiled. "Then there's nothing to worry about, is there?"

"My mama would never forgive me," said Faleesha.

"Your mother knows?"

"No!" said Faleesha, with alarm. "Don't tell her, please! It would kill her if she found out. Besides..." a tiny muscle in her left cheek twitched. "Vince said if I ever told Mama, he'd..." Faleesha hesitated, then pressed her lips shut.

"Well, then!" said Ms. Knowlton. "What your mother doesn't know —"

"My mama told me if I ever was to go and do something like this behind her back, Jesus would still know."

"Of course Jesus will know about your abortion," said Ms. Knowlton immediately. "And he will heartily approve!"

Faleesha looked up, incredulous. "How can you say that?"

"Why, through my spirit guide, of course," said Ms. Knowlton. "You couldn't possibly understand the significance of this, but I was once introduced to Lazaris, the greatest spirit master of them all. It was he who solved the puzzle of the true Jesus for me."

The older woman steepled her fingers together. "Do you know who Jesus really was, my child? He was an enlightened teacher who became such a perfect channel for his spirit guide that he was ages ahead of most of us. He instinctively knew he was God...something many of us are just now discovering about ourselves."

"If you say so," said Faleesha. "But I'm still afraid —"

"Listen to me," said Ms. Knowlton. "Abortion isn't right or wrong. It just is. There is no right or wrong. Whatever is, is right. It's your choice, don't you see? And Jesus is pro-choice! He knows you couldn't begin to have your stepfather's baby — so Jesus wants you to get an abortion."

"That's not what my mama would say," mumbled Faleesha. She lowered her voice, not sure she wanted the older woman to hear. "Her preacher tells everybody it...it's murder."

"Preachers!" exploded Colin Knowlton. "Preachers, ministers, television evangelists — they're all alike. Money-hungry vultures, every last one of them! They will enslave innocent people like your mother with any lie they can concoct."

The director's hanging glasses rose and fell with each breath. "But do their puritanical illusions of evil improve people's lives? No. All they do is make the poor poorer and the rich richer. Take my word for it,

Faleesha. People like that — all they want is your money."

Faleesha had often wondered privately about what she had just heard Ms. Knowlton say out loud. "Well...the last time I went to church with Mama, they did pass the plate twice..." said Faleesha. She paused. "And the preacher's car —"

"Is twice as expensive as your mother's, am I right?"

"Mama rides the bus."

"That's what I'm talking about! But your mother continues to give away her hard-earned money every time that plate passes by, am I right?"

Slowly, Faleesha nodded.

"I rest my case." She waited. Then she let her hands fall to her lap and said, "Your entire future is at stake, Faleesha. Which of us are you going to trust — the preacher who frightens your mother into giving him her money...or me?"

The older woman rose and stood beside Faleesha. She reached down and took Faleesha's left hand. Faleesha looked up. "Faleesha, Honey — every morning when I drive to work I risk my life, not knowing when some anti-abortionist maniac is going to point his gun at me.

"And when I arrive at the clinic, do you know what I do? All day long, I help girls just like you. They have nowhere else to turn. I have the power to make their problems go away. And I exercise that power! When they leave, they have new hope and a brighter future.

"But Faleesha —" the older woman cupped her hand under Faleesha's chin and stared directly into her eyes, "I never, ever, lie to them."

The director held her gaze for a long moment, then returned to her chair. She took a deep breath. "Yes. We must charge for our services. But would you like to know what I do with the profits? After my needs are met, I pour every last dime into the ministry of the Angel of Light Church — which, I am proud to say, I helped to found.

"Unlike your mother's church, we do not pressure the poor into making donations they can ill-afford. Instead, we raise their sights until they are able to see the dawning of a New Age...and then we gently guide them toward the Light."

Faleesha sat still.

"Which of us will it be, Faleesha? Whom do you trust?"

Faleesha hesitated, but only a moment. "You."

Colin Knowlton smiled. "Good. Now come with me. You have papers to sign. Then you can go get changed."

5

Faleesha lay on her back on the hard, narrow table. The rough sheet had been pushed up to her chest. Her bare feet squirmed in the cold obstetrical stirrups.

This isn't fair, she thought. Vince should be the one lying here on his back with his legs spread, not me. Her lower lip quivered.

"Just relax," said the doctor. "First I have to numb your cervix. You may feel a slight prick."

Faleesha let out a yelp of pain.

"Hold still, now," said the doctor. "Keep your feet in the stirrups. Trust me, young lady — you don't want to have any feeling down there when I insert the rods to dilate your cervix. Just two more pricks. Take a deep breath..."

After administering the shots, the doctor left the room. Faleesha felt so alone. She began to cry.

Fifteen minutes later, the doctor hurried back in, snapping on a new pair of surgical gloves. "Good and numb?" He picked up a long rod.

"Will the baby feel any—"

"It's not a baby!" said the doctor. "Didn't Colin explain all this to you? It's nothing more than a few cells of amorphous tissue attached to the inside of your uterus."

The doctor reached up and adjusted the hanging light. "You're what — not even a month late? You have nothing to worry about. Piece of cake. I doubt there will be any placenta to scrape. Now, relax!" he said. "First the rods..."

Faleesha felt the invasion and writhed on the table.

"There's no pain, is there?"

Faleesha shook her head no.

"Just discomfort?"

She nodded.

"One second more...you're doing great...there! That wasn't so bad, was it?"

Faleesha panted. Her hands gripped the metal bars on either side of the table.

"Calm down, now. Slow, deep breaths...that's it. The worst part is over. We're almost through." The doctor picked up the suction instrument and flipped a switch. The loud noise of a machine filled the room. "You won't feel a thing."

6

Her body stiff, Faleesha dressed slowly. Once the doctor had begun, the ordeal hadn't been nearly as bad as she had feared. It was over almost before she knew it. Surprisingly, there was very little pain.

Faleesha felt relieved. Now, maybe, she could go back to being a teenager again. That is, if Vince would let her.

At the front counter, the receptionist gave her a form to sign. "Is Ms. Knowlton still here?" asked

Faleesha. "I...I'd like to thank her for..."

"Oh, I'm sorry," said the receptionist. "You just missed her. She had to leave early to take the Mercedes in for repairs."

Faleesha laid down the pen. She frowned. "Did you say —"

"But I'll give her the message," said the receptionist. "That will be three hundred dollars. Ms. Knowlton said you would probably be paying cash?"

"Oh! Yes," said Faleesha, still thinking about Ms. Knowlton's car. "I'm sorry, I forgot. My purse...I think I left it in her office. Is...is it okay to go in and get it?"

The phone rang. "Women's Health Services," answered the receptionist, "Jeanette speaking — how may I help you?" She motioned for Faleesha to go on in.

7

Faleesha slowly opened the door and felt along the wall for a light switch, but couldn't find it. She poked her head out to ask the receptionist, but she was still on the phone.

The light from the waiting room helped a little, so Faleesha swung the door open as wide as it would go. She walked slowly into the dark office. Faleesha could just make out the shape of a lamp on the left-hand corner of Ms. Knowlton's desk. She felt around its smooth base, located the metal button and turned the lamp on. There! That was better.

Faleesha found her purse on the floor beside the chair, where she had dropped it. She unzipped the middle pocket. The money was still there — the roll of dirty bills bound tightly with a rubber band, just as he had handed it to her this morning.

Was it only this morning? It seemed such a long time ago that she had stumbled down the back steps of her home, Vince's threats ringing in her ears.

Faleesha sighed. "A Mercedes." Still, Ms. Knowlton had been kind. She really cares, thought Faleesha. Why else would she have taken so much time with me?

She zipped her purse shut and walked around the back side of the desk to turn off the lamp. Faleesha glanced down, the crystal pyramid still on top of the desk where Ms. Knowlton had placed it during their talk. It glittered brightly. How beautiful it was, thought Faleesha.

She paused and gently touched the point of the pyramid. She stroked the smooth surface along one side. Perhaps Ms. Knowlton's pyramid really did have mystical powers. She sure could use some now. Faleesha looked at the door. The waiting room was still empty. The receptionist was out of her line of sight.

Holding her breath, Faleesha reached forward with both hands and reverently lifted the fragile piece from the desk. Glancing again toward the door to be sure she was alone, she brought the pyramid close to her chest and closed her eyes.

What was it Ms. Knowlton had said? Something about vibrations of God. Faleesha concentrated as hard as she knew how. She squeezed the pyramid until its sharp edges bit painfully into her palms. She frowned and opened her eyes.

Nothing.

Maybe she was doing it wrong, she chided herself. Did the pyramid come with instructions? Faleesha scanned the desk. The pink sheet caught her attention. Was it hers?

Yes. There was her name, misspelled "Felicia," as usual. Why did people always do that? Then the false address she had given them, along with the wrong age.

Vince had told her to put down wrong information so no one could trace her to him.

She skimmed through several paragraphs she didn't understand down to the bottom of the sheet. "CARDS Test administered to determine the presence of HCG in patient's urine," it said. "A positive finding indicates the patient is pregnant."

There was one more line after that.

Faleesha let out a tiny squeal. The crystal pyramid fell from her limp fingers and shattered on the floor.

Hands trembling, Faleesha raised the pink sheet to her face and stared at the bottom line in shocked disbelief.

Results of Pregnancy Test: NEGATIVE

WHY A CHURCH MEMBER WON'T GO

*She sat among us, at the best,
A not unfeared, half-welcome guest*
—John Greenleaf Whittier

1

No one spoke.
Perched on one corner of her flowered sofa, Kathy's eyes widened. How could ten people crammed into a single living room all manage to avoid looking at the other nine? Kathy shook her head slightly in reluctant admiration. In a room this tiny, that was quite a feat.
But right now that was the only thing she admired about her prominent, proper, oh-so-righteous family.
"Thank you all for coming," Kathy began.
At the sudden sound of her voice, three of them jerked as though she had slapped them. She would have liked to.

"I know this is a bad time for you — with tomorrow being such a big day, and all. And I know that nobody likes this sort of thing — it's just that I thought...especially at this time of year..."

Even though she was speaking, they refused to look at her. They still wouldn't look at each other, either. Before today, she hadn't realized how fascinating the pattern of her living room rug must be.

"Look," said Kathy, plunging in, "Jon is going to marry her. Last Monday night he asked Keteisha to be his wife, and she said yes."

Everyone stiffened.

"You all know she's black — or rather, African-American. I keep forgetting to say it right."

Her brother-in-law Ted rolled his eyes and exchanged glances with her bearded brother-in-law, Mike. Finally, somebody had looked at somebody else. Progress!

Well, sort of.

2

"I haven't asked you over to continue the debate about whether or not they should be dating," said Kathy. "It's gone beyond that now. Sometime this year there's going to be a wedding."

Her dad looked up and glared at her.

"The question is, now that it's a reality, where do we go from here? I mean, it's time to face it: In a couple of years, Mom and Dad, you're likely to have a bla — an African-American — great grandbaby."

Her dad groaned.

"You mean 'mixed,' " said her sister Jean.

"Well, yes," conceded Kathy. "But that's one of the points I wanted to make: we're ALL mixed! Grandpa was Irish-American. Grandma, you're mostly English — let's see, Mom, that makes you —"

"I will not have that child in my home!" barked her grandmother. "If they think for a moment that I will ever baby-sit that, that mixed-breed monstrosity, they had better think again."

" 'Mixed-breed monstrosity'?" echoed Kathy. The poor old woman was slipping. At her age, no one was about to ask her to baby-sit anybody. "Grandma! You're talking about your —"

"And you may as well know right now that I will not attend the wedding," said her father.

"Daddy —"

"Don't 'Daddy' me, young lady. You're not acting like any daughter of mine."

"I can't believe you said that," murmured Kathy. Tears sprang to her eyes. "Somebody please tell me this isn't happening."

"You're the one who wanted this meeting, not us," said Jean.

"Yes, but to work things out," said Kathy, "not to be tossed out of the family!"

"Nobody's tossing anybody out," said Carol, her younger sister. "That's ridiculous."

"Oh?" said Kathy, the tears flowing freely down her cheeks, now. "Does that mean Jon and Keteisha can come to your big dinner tomorrow?"

"That's not my place to say," replied Carol. "It's not my house."

"Well, if it were your house," said Kathy. "Would they be welcome then?"

"Jonathan is always welcome at my house, you know that."

"I'm talking about Jon *and* Keteisha," said Kathy. "They're engaged. Are my son and his fiancee welcome in your house?"

Carol glanced nervously at Carol's husband Mike, who avoided her gaze.

"Is the young woman who is about to become my daughter-in-law welcome in any of your homes?"

Kathy persisted.

All eyes resumed their study of her carpet.

She looked at her brother Barry, whom she had counted on to take her side. He sat silently beside his wife.

"Barry?" Kathy prodded.

"I'm sorry, Sis. Margie and I have talked. It really doesn't have anything to do with us. It's about the kids. If Jon is allowed to bring his girlfriend to family gatherings, then Amy and Jeff are going to think we approve of interracial dating. We know how you feel, Kathy, but...we really don't want to send them that message."

Kathy shook her head. Barry had delivered his speech without looking at her once. Her little brother. Times beyond counting she had stayed at home and baby-sat him, instead of going out and having a good time. He adored her! Didn't he?

"C'mon, Kathy," broke in Jean. "Cut us some slack. You'd feel the same way, if you were in our shoes! If we don't show our kids there's a price to be paid for dating out of their race, the same thing could happen to us that has happened to you. We can't let this come into our family. We have to stop it here."

"Maybe I don't have a right to speak, since I'm a son-in-law," blurted Ted, precariously shifting his 240-pound bulk around on the too-small chair she had brought in from the kitchen. "But since Jean made me come tonight, I guess I'll speak my peace."

This ought to be good, thought Kathy. I wonder if he'll bring up the fifteen hundred dollars he and Jean still owe me, from when he was laid off from work and they almost lost their home. I was there for you, big guy. Are you and that ungrateful sister of mine going to be here for me?

"Kathy, I don't think you appreciate what a wonderful family you have, here. I came from a broken home. You all know my father was an alcoholic.

"When Jean and I got married, I became part of the most wholesome family in this city. You don't drink. You don't smoke. You don't even curse when you get mad. Twelve years ago, I wouldn't have believed such an ideal family even existed!"

Oh my God, thought Kathy, as she sank back against the couch. He's going for points. He sees which way the wind is blowing, and he's decided to ingratiate himself with the others — at my expense.

"Kathy, I don't mean this in any way as a put-down, but you're the only one of your family that has, well...stayed in the background. Oh, you go to church now and then, when you can work it in. But the rest of us — and I'm grateful to include myself in this — we're leaders! Other people look up to us!"

"That's right," chimed in Jean, who was leaning forward in her familiar, condescending manner. "Is it possible that the only one you're thinking of here, is yourself? The rest of us don't have that luxury. We have to consider how this will affect our entire church! What will other people think?"

" 'What will other people think?' " Kathy sat up. "Do You know what you all are?" Kathy's voice became shrill. "You're... you're —"

"— a bunch of racists," finished Jonathan.

3

They looked up to see Kathy's 21-year-old son, who stood in the living room doorway.

"How dare you call me a racist," snarled Kathy's dad. "I have plenty of blacks who work for me at the shop. I treat them the same as everyone else."

"That's right," snapped Jean. "You don't know what you're talking about, Jonathan. When our children have birthday parties, their black school friends always come. We think nothing of it."

"But you don't really let them inside," said Jonathan, pointing to the center of his chest. He strode to the middle of the room. "You make no attempt to connect with them as people."

"You're out of order, young man!" barked Kathy's father.

"Well, sir, I may be, but no more than you. This family has always given lip service to not being prejudiced. But do you want to hear something really funny? I believed you! When all of you mouthed those pious words about everybody being created equal, I bought it — hook, line and sinker!"

Kathy saw that her son's eyes were shining with an unusual brightness. Jonathan moved from one relative to another, cocking his head to one side until he caught their eyes and made them look at him. "Hey! Here's the real screamer, guys — you're the ones who taught me about race, in Sunday School. Remember this song? It's one of your favorites." Jonathan sang:

> Jesus loves the little children
> All the children of the world
> Red and yellow, black and white
> They are precious in His sight
> Jesus loves the little children of the world

"And guess what? You were right! They really are precious. But unlike you, I actually got to know one of them. And do you know what happened? I fell in love with her! All because of what you taught me, you phony hypocrites!"

"Now, just a cotton-pickin' minute," said Ted. "I resent being called a —"

"I'm not finished," said Jonathan. His eyes glistened with emotion. "I fell in love with her because she's a wonderful person. She's generous and good and sweet, and she loves me with all her heart.

The only reason you won't accept her is because she's black. That's why I called you a bunch of racists — because that's what you are."

"No, we are not!" shouted Kathy's mother and stood up.

4

Kathy and the others looked at Mrs. Campbell — surprised at the anger in her voice. Before today she had always been the peacemaker, the one who soothed things over. But now she shook with anger. Even though Jonathan had warned Kathy that her family would never accept this, Kathy could not believe the raw, red rage that now distorted her mother's face.

Mrs. Campbell walked toward Jonathan and poked a boney finger in his face. "You...are about to disgrace us all. First your mother with her divorce, and now this. Not only can't she keep a husband, she can't even control her own child!"

"You leave my mother out of this!" shouted Jonathan. "This is my choice — mine, and no one else's."

His grandmother stepped closer. "You're going through a phase, Jonathan. That's all. A phase. You're curious. You want to find out what a black girl is like. So go ahead and find out — get it out of your system."

She shoved her quivering face closer to Jonathan's. "But don't come dragging her in here to ruin our family! She doesn't belong here! She belongs back in the ghetto, with her kind."

Her voice lowered. "And don't you for one minute think you are going to march her down our church aisle in a white dress, do you hear me? She doesn't belong in a white dress. She's nothing but a nigger!"

5

The force of Jonathan's slap sent his grandmother reeling, arms flailing, to the floor.

The old woman lay there, next to her broken glasses. She moaned. Bending over her, Jonathan stammered, "Grandma, I'm —"

Bellowing with rage, Jonathan's grandfather hurtled into the body of his grandson in an awkward tackle that sent them sprawling onto the coffee table. One of its legs snapped and spilled them onto the floor.

"Dad! Jon! Stop it! Stop it this instant!" Kathy screamed.

Kathy's dad had landed on top. "Don't you ever touch my wife again!" he growled, his face an inch above Jonathan's. The old man's joints creaked as he slowly pushed himself to his knees, panting.

Jonathan crawled out from under his grandfather and lurched to his feet. His face contorted. "I hate you — all of you!" he sobbed. Jonathan staggered from the room and out the front door.

"Jon, wait!" Kathy called. She ran out of the house and down the sidewalk after him. Jonathan slammed his car door, gunned the engine and squealed away from the curb. Tears streamed down Kathy's cheeks as she watched her son speed away.

6

Kathy stepped back inside and closed the front door after her. She walked into the living room and saw her family standing in a silent circle around Mrs. Campbell.

With the help of Carol and Jean, the old woman slowly rose to her feet. Barry handed his mother her broken glasses. She put them on, gingerly adjusting the crooked frame above the bright red spot on her left cheek.

"Do you see?" she said at last, in a shaky voice. "Do you see where this mixing of the races leads? Shame, Katherine! For shame!"

"Shame on me?" Kathy said. "No, Mother! Shame on you! The mixing of the races didn't do this — you did! You insulted the girl my son loves and chased him out of his own home!"

"He's not the only one who's been chased off," said Kathy's dad. "Where are our coats?"

"No, please," pleaded Kathy. She hadn't wanted a family split. She had wanted everybody to calmly sit down together and work things out. Don't leave like this. We've got to somehow —"

"Not me," said Jean. "You promised us Jonathan wouldn't be here. But you lied! Not only did you turn him loose on us, but you stood by while he physically assaulted our mother!"

"That's not fair!" Kathy cried. "I swear to you that I didn't know Jon was coming — I didn't even think he knew about the meeting. And I would never condone —"

"Sis, it's late," interrupted Barry. He shifted his weight from foot to foot. "Why don't we call it a night? In case you're forgetting, we've all got to get up really early in the morning."

"Oh, that's right!" Kathy said. "For a moment, there, I had almost forgotten. How insensitive of me. This is Saturday night, isn't it?"

In a daze, Kathy followed her mother and father to the front door. "You have to be there for sunrise service at 6:00, don't you, Daddy? You're chairman of the deacon board. You always offer the opening prayer."

"Yes, he does, Katherine," said her mother. "He's been working on it all week. He's read it to me several times, and it's beautiful. So don't be late."

Kathy watched her mother lean on her father's arm, as they hobbled down the sidewalk. "You know..." she called after them, "...you...better not look for me — I don't think I'm going to be able to make it."

Kathy's father stopped. He wheeled around and pointed his finger at Kathy. "You need to be in church tomorrow morning, Young Lady!"

Kathy stared at her father's stern face. Then she closed the door.

7

The others had moved into the foyer behind her. As she turned around she saw that they were slipping into their coats. "So," said Kathy. "You're leaving, too."

"Yes," said Jean. "We have to go home and get the kids in bed. They've got —"

"— to get up early tomorrow," said Kathy. "Yes. I believe that's already been pointed out to me."

Jean sighed and shook her head. "Grandmother? Are you ready? Let's go. Ted, help her with her coat, will you?"

Kathy watched silently as the three of them left.

Marge and Barry were next. At the door, Barry leaned over and gave Kathy a peck on the cheek. "Don't be upset with us, Sis. We...we just want what's best. That's all. I'm sorry that...well, that things didn't...you know." He shrugged. "I guess this is...good night, then. You take care of yourself, you hear?"

And they left.

"Night, Kathy," said Mike, as he walked out the door. He didn't look at her. On his way down the sidewalk, he called over his shoulder. "Carol? You coming?"

"In a minute," she answered. "You go ahead. I'll be right there."

Carol faced her sister and took Kathy's hands. "Are you going to be all right?"

Kathy nodded.

"Kath — you didn't mean it, did you — what you said to Daddy? About not coming to hear him read his prayer in the morning?"

The two women searched each other's eyes. "I think so," said Kathy. "After all this...I'm sorry. I just don't think I'm up to it."

"It'll hurt him."

"He hurt me."

Carol looked down at their hands. "I know."

Kathy pulled away. "Mike's waiting. You'd better go." Kathy turned and walked into the living room. She bent down and picked up several magazines that had fallen from the broken coffee table.

"You will be there for the main service at 11:00, won't you?"

Surprised, Kathy looked up to see Carol standing in the doorway of the living room. "I thought you'd left."

"You will be there then, right?"

The magazines slid from Kathy's fingers and hit the floor. Kathy buried her face in her hands and wept.

Carol walked over and put a hand on her big sister's shoulder. "What? What did I say?"

Kathy lifted her tearstained face. "What is it with this family? Our lives are falling apart, and all you people can do is pressure me to show up for church!"

"It's not just any Sunday, Kathy," said Carol. "It's Easter! Tomorrow morning is all about resurrection and happiness and life! It's the biggest day of the year."

Kathy closed her eyes and shook her head.

"It's also about family," said Carol, squeezing

Kathy's shoulder. "None of us has ever missed church on Easter Sunday. You know that. When we all sit together, we fill up two whole pews! It's who we are, it's what we do. It's our family tradition."

"Not this time," said Kathy, turning away. "For you, maybe. But not for me. You'll just have to celebrate Easter without me, this year."

"And how is that going to look to the rest of the church?" cried Carol. "Everybody will know you're missing. People will talk. They'll ask questions. They'll want to know where you are — if you're sick, if you're having problems. What are we supposed to tell them?"

Kathy walked to the window and peered out in the direction her son had gone. She did not turn around.

"Tell them..." Kathy paused.

"Tell them...there's been a death in the family."

THOUGH A MURDERER MIGHT!

WHY A "BORN-AGAIN" PERSON WON'T GO

*In the desert
I saw a creature, naked, bestial,
Who, squatting upon the ground,
Held his heart in his hands,
And ate of it.
I said, "Is it good, friend?"
"It is bitter — bitter," he answered,
"But I like it
Because it is bitter,
And because it is my heart."*

—Stephen Crane

1

Alex slapped the alarm clock, trying to stop the noise so he could go back to sleep.

The ringing continued.

Lessee...must be the phone. Yeah. S'prob'ly the phone. Better answer it.

"Yeah?"

The voice on the other end was low, warm and sexy. "Hey, Big Man."

Alex woke up. Tammy. She was the only one who called him that. It was her pet name for him, and she knew exactly what hearing it did to him.

"Hey, Baby — what's up?" Alex wiped the sleep from his eyes.

"I can tell you're not."

"Don't dog on me, girl. I got to bed late last night."

"I don't think I want to hear about it," said Tammy, sounding irritated.

"Naw, naw! Nothin' like that. I was just layin' here eatin,' watchin' TV, killin' time — y'know?"

"I'll bet."

"I swear!" And it was the truth. His social life stank lately.

"Okay, okay, I believe you," said Tammy, the purr back in her voice. "So...do you still know how to take a lady out to dinner and show her a good time?"

"You know I do, Sugar." Alex frowned. "So what's the story with Tommy?"

"Tommy who?" she laughed.

"Tommy and Tammy, the hottest number in town for the last two-three months — that's the 'Tommy Who!'"

"Oh, him! Yes, well...let's just say every puppy eventually opens her eyes."

"Took you long enough."

"Don't be mad at me, Alex," murmured Tammy. "I'm willing to make it up to you."

"Uh-huh," said Alex. This could be good. "What year?"

"How about this year?"

"What month?"

"How about this month?" she continued, playing

the game.

"What day, then?" said Alex, trying not to sound too eager.

"Who said anything about 'day?' Big Man," whispered Tammy. "I'm talking about tonight."

There is a God, thought Alex. "I dunno. Have to check my calendar."

"You mean your TV Guide?"

"I'm gonna ignore that. See, here's the problem — it's Friday night, and I got this big party I'm s'posed to go to..."

"So take me with you."

"But! — I'm not finished, girl, don't interrupt me, now — but...I'm willing to cancel my plans to be with you."

"Oh, now," said Tammy, "isn't that sweet. But I wouldn't think of asking you to miss your party."

"Hey! Who's to say you and me can't have a better party — just the two of us?"

"Not me, Big Man," said Tammy. "We've had some good times."

"Yeah," said Big Man, remembering. "Some really good times. So! You want to do dinner and the whole thing, huh?"

"That's right," said Tammy. "The whole thing."

"Pick you up 'bout eight?"

"I'll be waiting."

Yeah, me too, thought Alex, as he hung up the phone. How long has it been? Well, hang in there just a few more hours, Big Man. Tonight's the night.

He sniffed under both arms. Better shower.

2

Alex pulled away from the curb and helped himself to an eyeful of Tammy in her red mini-skirt, her legs angled toward him in the cramped confines of his aging red sports car.

"Nice skirt," said Alex.

"You weren't looking at my skirt," Tammy smiled. "And keep your eyes on the road. I'm hungry and I want to get there in one piece."

"Are you sure you want to take the time to go to a restaurant?" said Alex. "I mean, if you're that hungry, we could grab some take-out, go on over to my place and —"

"Alex, you promised to take me to dinner."

"And I'm gonna! I was just sayin' that if —"

"I know what you were saying. Patience, Big Man, patience."

Alex let out a lungful of air and slid down in the driver's seat. He punched the gas.

3

"So this is why you wanted to go to dinner with me tonight — to tell me you got religion?" Alex waved the waitress away. Not now. She could wait for her money.

"Well...yes, partly," said Tammy, looking at him anxiously.

"Why did you go and do somethin' like that?" demanded Alex. This was not good news. No sir. Not good at all. "I mean, you and Tommy had that many problems, or what?"

"This doesn't have anything to do with Tommy."

"Well, what then?" said Alex. "Whaddaya — goin' to church?"

"Yes, I am, Alex," replied Tammy. "Does that bother you?"

"No," Alex lied. "It's just that, y'know, I didn't picture you for the type, that's all."

"What's that supposed to mean?"

"You know."

"No, I don't," Tammy raised her voice. "Do you want to spell it out for me?"

"Ah...no," retreated Alex. "I didn't mean nothin' by it. I just — y'know, it's awful sudden, isn't it? I mean, last I knew, you couldn't have cared less about church."

"That's true!" said Tammy. "But that's not how it started. About a month ago, these people came to my door, taking a religious survey."

"Yeah," said Alex, "them Watchtower people. They bug me all the time, too."

"No, silly, I wouldn't have talked to them. This was different. I knew one of them — a girl I used to go to school with — so I let them in."

"You let them in," echoed Alex, nodding his head disgustedly, as though she had committed the biggest blunder of her life. "Did they hit you up for the money then, or later?"

"Alex, it wasn't like that! It wasn't like that, at all. They were very polite. All they wanted was to ask me a few questions — for their survey."

"Questions. Yeah, right. Such as —?"

"Well, did I go to church, did I believe in God, did I agree with the Ten Commandments — things like that."

"And you started going to church just because some old girlfriend of yours got nosey with your personal life?"

"No, just listen. They said they had only one more question for me, and then they would be through."

"That should've tipped you off to somethin,' right there."

"Alex!"

"Okay, okay."

"Anyway, she wanted to know if I died that night, if I was sure I would go to heaven."

"Oh, Lord. I would've told her right then that it was none of her cotton-pickin' —"

"And I told her the truth, Alex. I told her no, I didn't."

"Don't you see, girl?" Alex broke in again. "It was a set-up! Nobody can know somethin' like that. You go walkin' into a trap like that — now they got you where they want you."

"Alex, please. This girl I went to school with — Karen's her name — she had such a glow about her, such a —"

"Yeah, 'a glow.' She was probably on somethin.' "

"Actually, you're right," said Tammy. "She was on Jesus."

"Jesus Christ!" cursed Alex.

"Exactly!" said Tammy. "She told me that the neat thing about her life was that she knew she was going to heaven. And then she asked me if I wanted her to tell me how I could know for sure that I was going to heaven, too."

Alex shook his head in confusion and started to fiddle with his soiled napkin. This was too deep for him — not to mention depressing. He had just blown thirty-five bucks on dinner for a girl who wasn't going to —

"So, she went ahead to tell me that I was a sinner."

"And one of the best, too," muttered Alex.

"What did you say?"

"Nothin.' I didn't say nothin.' "

"Anyway, she said Jesus died on the cross to pay for all my sins."

"All of 'em? That's quite a deal, girl. In fact, I'd call it the deal of the century."

"Alex, stop teasing. She told me Jesus did all that so I wouldn't have to die and go to hell. Come on — isn't that neat?"

Alex looked up from his napkin and studied her a moment before answering. In spite of himself, he had to admit something different was going on here.

"Yeah," he said. "That's neat. So then, what

happened? You joined the church next Sunday, or what?"

"No! So then Karen asked me if I wanted to become a Christian, and I said yes. She gave me a little prayer to pray, and I did. And then she told me I was born again."

Alex stared. "You're really serious with this, aren't you?"

Tammy nodded. "You know what I did when she told me I was going to heaven?"

"No, what'd you do?"

"I cried."

Alex couldn't believe his ears. Here was this girl who used to be the wildest thing he had ever tried to tame, telling him that she had turned her back on all that and switched to Jesus. What a waste! But as soon as he thought that, he felt guilty. Hey, Tommy was one thing. But Jesus? He didn't begin to know how he could compete with that Dude.

"Man," Alex said, shaking his head. "If this don't beat all. Man." Alex reached for a toothpick and leaned back in his chair. Tammy watched in silence as he thought and picked his teeth.

Two tables away, a busboy dropped his tray of dishes. The loud clatter made Tammy jump. Alex didn't notice. He usually thought about one thing at a time. And Tammy had given him something to think about that required every bit of brain power he had to give to it.

The busboy had the mess half cleaned up when Alex pulled the toothpick out of his mouth and pointed it at her. "Well, girl, I gotta admire you. Normally, I hate religious types, 'cause if there's one thing I can't stand, it's one of them holy-roller hypocrites, you know what I'm sayin'?

"Sure, I know."

"But you...you're for real, I can tell that. And I, uh, y'know, I respect you for that."

There. He had said it. And as soon as he had, he felt, well, righteous, somehow. Like he'd dropped a buck in the Salvation Army kettle, or something.

After all, he had just been nice to a girl that, as it turns out, wasn't going to do one blessed thing for him.

He stood up, then, and threw down enough money to cover the bill. Alex looked at Tammy and smiled a protective smile, kind of like he would have at his sister, if he had one.

"Ready to go?" he asked, helping her with her coat for the first time since he had known her.

4

Alex started to unlock his car door, then stopped, his key two inches from the lock. Without quite understanding why, he walked around and opened the car door for Tammy. He even averted his eyes when she swung her legs inside.

"Tell me what you're thinking," Tammy said, after they had driven for a while in silence.

Alex snorted, not about to reveal his thoughts. He was thinking that he had showered for nothing, if she really wanted to know.

"Are you upset with me?" Tammy asked.

"Nah." It was almost true. He had no right to be mad at her for trying to do something good with her life — even if it meant he should have taken a cold shower, instead of a hot one.

"If you're not upset, why are you so quiet?"

"You surprised me, that's all."

"I thought you liked surprises."

"I do," said Alex. "But this was more like a shock."

"I don't see why. A lot of people get born-again."

"Yeah, but it's not as big a change."

"You think I've changed?"

"Oh, yeah," said Alex.

"How?"

"You're...just different, that's all. It's hard to say." Brother, was it hard to say.

"Would you say I've changed for the better?"

Alex decided to think that one over, before answering. Better for him? No. Terrible for him. But what about Tammy? She was giving up a lot. Too much, as far as he was concerned. But if it made her happier...

"Hey — if it works for you then, yeah — I guess it's...better," said Alex.

He checked his rear view mirror and took the service road that emptied onto the bypass. As he merged left into heavy traffic, a question popped into Alex's mind. "Tell me somethin' — have you let anybody else from the old gang in on your...you know, the thing that you did?"

"Oh, sure! I've told almost everybody — Karen, Melissa, Dan — and guess what? Julie's started going to church with me!"

Alex's jaw dropped. Julie? In church? She had been wilder than Tammy. What was going on, here?

"You've got that look on your face again. Are you sure you're not mad at me?"

"Nope," said Alex. "Actually...aw, I was just thinkin'. This is really somethin' — you tellin' everybody, not bein' ashamed of it, and all. Takes guts. Kinda restores my faith in mankind."

"Don't you mean womankind?" Tammy said playfully.

"Whatever — now don't start with that!" Alex laughed. "You've worked on me enough tonight!"

"That's what you think," said Tammy. "I'm just getting warmed up!"

Alex shot her a wary glance. If she planned to try to convert him tonight, she was in for one severe disappointment. The evening was over, as far as he was concerned.

As Alex took the next exit, Tammy asked where he was going.

"I'm taking you home, little girl."

"Alex, we can't. I have a roommate, remember? Let's go to your place."

She was turning into a fanatic. Better dump her, fast. "I'm sorry, Tammy, gotta take a rain check. Guess I'm just all talked out tonight."

"So, who said anything about talk?" murmured Tammy, as she reached over and placed her hand on his knee.

Alex slowed the car, pulled onto a side street along the curb, shifted into neutral and jerked the emergency brake. "What's going on?"

"I promised I would make it up to you, Baby — remember? Do you want me to say how? Is that it? Does Big Man want to hear me say it?"

"Say what? Hey, girl — I thought you got religion."

Tammy leaned closer and blew in his left ear. "What does that have to do with anything?"

"I thought you born-again types didn't...didn't — you know."

"No, I don't, Alex. Tell me — what don't we born-again types do?" Tammy giggled. "Don't we do this?" She whispered the word in his ear. "Or what about this?" She whispered again.

Alex pulled away. "Hey! What gives with you? Tell me I'm not hearin' this!"

"Why are you so uptight, Alex? All I said was —"

"I heard what you said. See, that's the trouble. I heard what you said both times — in the restaurant and just now, sittin' here next to me."

"Hey, Big Man..." Tammy leaned over to brush his cheek with her lips. He could feel her warmth. He could smell her perfume. "...let's get something straight. I agreed to go to Heaven — not to a convent."

Alex knew he should have been relieved. He hadn't showered in vain, after all. He knew he should have been excited. It had been such a long, long time. But he was stunned to find that he was neither of those things. All he felt was sick inside.

Alex gripped the top of the steering wheel with both hands and let his head drop between his knotted biceps. His lips compressed into a tight line.

Without a glance at Tammy, Alex eased the emergency brake forward, shifted into first and pulled away from the curb.

One turn. Two.

"Alex, this isn't the way to your apartment."

"No," replied Alex, a muscle working in his jaw. "It isn't."

WHY A CLERGYMAN WON'T GO

*Yet not for all his faith can see
Would I that cowled churchman be*

—William Cullen Bryant

1

Eight minutes had passed, but Martha continued to wait patiently for the department store sales associate to finish with her customer. Clutching the package of pantyhose she intended to purchase, Martha made sure she was standing back, discreetly off to one side, so as not to pressure the two ladies as they transacted their business.

Martha did not consider clearing her throat for attention or frowning impatiently, even though this unexpected delay was about to make her late for her appointment with Reverend Thomas. Her mother had reared her to believe that a person of good breeding never openly conveyed annoyance, no matter how much personal turmoil had to be suppressed.

To compound her inner discomfort, she felt ill. Am I running a temperature? she wondered, stifling the impulse to touch her cheeks and forehead. I must be coming down with the flu.

Martha tried not to eavesdrop, but the sales associate had a voice that carried.

"Wait!" the woman said to her customer. "Before you go, you have to let me show you something we just got in. Take a whiff of this." She sprayed a small cotton ball and wafted it underneath her customer's nostrils.

"Ugh!" the woman exclaimed, recoiling. "That's atrocious! What is it?"

"Evel Cologne," laughed the sales associate. "And believe it or not, we can't keep it in stock. It's our number one-selling men's fragrance."

"But why?" the customer asked. "That is positively the most offensive — well, it smells like...like..."

"Urine."

"That's it — that's it, exactly! Why would any man in his right mind buy a bottle of cologne that makes him smell like he's just wet all over himself?"

"Haven't you heard the commercials?" asked the sales associate. 'Evel Cologne contains a powerful male hormone that makes women want to hurl themselves at your feet.' "

"It makes me want to hurl, all right!" said the customer, and both women laughed.

Martha didn't laugh but was in desperate agreement. When the sales associate sprayed the cotton ball, she had pointed the bottle in Martha's direction. One whiff of the odoriferous mist was all it took. Her eyes widened because of the violent reaction in her stomach.

Martha no longer cared that she had a runner in her hose. She left her intended purchase on the glass counter and quickly walked away, fighting the urge to cup her hand over her mouth.

"Ms.? Oh, Ms.!" cried the sales associate after her. "May I help you?"

Mortified by the rude haste of her exit, Martha nevertheless did not trust herself to pause or open her mouth to explain. She had to get air. Now. Without a backward glance, she bolted down the crowded aisle and out the huge glass door.

2

Thank God. She made it.

Martha deeply inhaled the crisp air. Her nausea subsided. She had come within a whisker of — no. Don't think about it. It might happen yet.

Beads of cold perspiration dotted her forehead, giving her a chill. She wondered if she looked as pale as she felt.

"Are you all right?" A man's voice startled her.

"Yes, of course," Martha replied automatically. "I just...that is, I..." This is so embarrassing, she thought.

"Would you like me to get you a cab?" the stranger persisted. "You really don't look too well."

"No, that's...not necessary," Martha replied. Now she felt weak, dizzy. "I can get a cab...in just a moment. I'm just a little..."

"Taxi!" the man yelled. A battered yellow cab darted across two lanes of traffic and pulled alongside the curb.

"This woman's not feeling well," the man told the driver. He opened the door for Martha. "You might want to see if she needs to go to the hospital." Then he shut the door, slowly backed away from the cab, and peered at her through the dirty window.

"Where to, lady?" rasped the unshaven cab driver.

Head bowed, eyes closed, Martha raised one hand

to request a moment to regain her composure. The cabbie shrugged, and flipped on his meter.

I'm too sick to keep this appointment, she thought. I need to go home and get into bed. But I can't do that, she scolded herself. I'm due there in fifteen minutes. He's a busy man. I can't just not show up. What would he think of me?

Martha steeled herself and slowly forced open her eyes. To the cab driver she said in a shaky voice, "1100 Canal Street. It's the church there — St. Michael's."

For the first time in her life, Martha was going to counsel with a minister.

Martha's parents were both atheists. They would be horrified if they knew where she was headed. This was, she reflected with no small amount of guilt, the first step of any consequence she had ever taken without their knowledge and approval.

Her work as a legal secretary gave her no satisfaction. The daily jumble of plea bargains, cash settlements and quiet deals behind the scenes had long ago burned out the naive respect she had once held for the law.

She lived alone. There was no one in her life, man or woman. Men wearied her. She was tired of being pawed. Women were nosey, constantly prying into her affairs, trying to get at her inner thoughts, her emotions. It was none of their business. One way or the other, every person she had ever known for any length of time had sooner or later attempted an invasion of her privacy.

Except her parents. They had always respected her personhood. They had kept their distance.

Martha shivered. She pulled her coat tightly about her. Why is it so cold in here? she wondered. Then she noticed that the cab driver seemed quite comfortable — he wore only a flannel shirt. She looked again. A filthy flannel shirt. Maybe it isn't

cold in the cab, she decided. Maybe it's just me.
Unlike her parents, Martha was not a committed atheist. She had no feeling about God one way or the other. He seemed an abstract concept that she had merely filed away along with other conundrums she had no desire to think about, like quantum mechanics or quarks.
She wasn't completely sure what drew her to attend her first church service four weeks ago. Perhaps she had lost her belief in disbelief. And why not? The irreligion of her parents wasn't working for her. By contrast, millions of people apparently found some solace in the practice of mystic forms and ancient traditions.
She did know why she had selected St. Michael's, however. The building itself had been erected several centuries ago. Located in the oldest part of the city, its soaring twin spires represented solidity. Permanence. Refuge.
She envisioned that a person who valued her privacy could quietly slip in and hide in one of its hard, dark pews in the back. Unnoticed within its dimly-lit cavernous sanctuary, she would be free to merely observe, unmolested.
Two things had surprised her about that first service. One was the sparse crowd. Only about a hundred people were scattered here and there throughout the great room, which could have easily accommodated six or seven times that many. She found a pew to herself. The nearest person was twenty feet away. She liked that.
The other surprise was the minister. Braced to defend herself against an all-out assault of fear and superstition, she was struck instead by the worldly sophistication of his remarks. "Let us once and for all extinguish the fire and brimstone of our barbaric past," he had said. "And let us quench the flames of intimidation with the cool, refreshing waters of peace,

calm and utter serenity — an infinitely higher way of life that tastes of heaven on earth."

As he concluded his remarks, Martha was pleased. Reverend Thomas had made his appeal to the intellect, rather than to base emotion. His words had touched her mind and left her heart alone.

Although the crashing chords of the pipe organ reminded her of the soundtrack from a 1940's horror movie, the service was not an unpleasant experience. She was not the only one who didn't recite, kneel, donate, sing or participate in the other peculiar rituals that were conducted with such dignity and solemnity. No one bothered her. No one so much as walked up to say hello. Reassured, she decided to return.

On the following week, the minister's sermon impressed her once again. As she watched him speak, she decided that she liked his backwards collar and black robe. "I am not like other men," it seemed to say. "I have risen above their fleshly passions and chosen to serve humankind, rather than debase it."

On her third visit, she realized what she liked most about Reverend Thomas. He wanted nothing from her. He expected nothing of her. He merely presented rational concepts for her consideration that she could take or leave. The choice was entirely up to her. He was the first person who had ever made her feel completely safe.

On her way out of the building, Martha noticed several left-over church bulletins in the rack beside the door. Curious, she took one home with her. The first three pages of the bulletin contained little of interest to her. But on the back, down at the bottom, there was a small box that caught her attention. Reverend Thomas had posted counseling hours, it said, within which time one could make an appointment.

She thought about that all week.

Yesterday she called the church office — only to

obtain additional information, she told herself. Yes, Reverend Thomas counseled non-members. That was commendable, she thought. No, he did not charge a fee. Really? That was unexpected. In fact, the woman told her, they had just received a cancellation. There was an immediate opening. Could Martha come in tomorrow afternoon at 4:00?

Her inner self warned her to back away, to buy more time — but her outer self seemed powerless to resist. In a daze, she listened to a voice quite similar to hers acknowledge that an appointment had just been set.

3

As the secretary showed her into his office, Reverend Thomas stood and invited Martha to be seated. She sat down in a solid oak armchair that felt as though it had been worn smooth by a continual stream of troubled people before her.

Reverend Thomas looked different. Instead of his pulpit robe, he wore a less formal black suit coat over a black shirt. The white backwards collar, however, was still in place, Martha noted with relief. Adding to her sense of safety was the mammoth desk that provided a protective barrier between them.

"How may I help you?" Reverend Thomas asked. He leaned back, making his desk chair emit a loud creak.

It's too hot in here, thought Martha. I wish he would open a window. She looked around the small room. There were no windows. No wonder the air in here was so stale.

"It is 'Martha,' isn't it?" Reverend Thomas asked.

She nodded. He's waiting for me to say something, she thought. "Actually, I'm not feeling too well," she began, and immediately felt foolish for saying it. He was a minister, not a medical doctor.

"Something is troubling you..." Reverend Thomas nodded, encouraging her to continue. His brow knitted with concern and he leaned forward, making the chair creak again.

What a kind, compassionate man, Martha thought. He's trying to help me with my spiritual questions, while all I can do is think about my queasy stomach. I must not squander this opportunity. I can be sick later. "Yes...there is something," said Martha.

She paused. Could she do this? As far back as Martha could remember, she had never opened herself to another person. The prospect terrified her.

But something else frightened her even more: the daily agony of carrying her haunting questions, unresolved, all the way to her grave. If she could not seek counsel from a person so caring as Reverend Thomas — then from whom?

She was here. She had come this far. She had to take the next step. Martha took a deep breath. "I don't believe in God," she said. "What I mean to say is...I think, at this point in my life, that I would like to believe in a divine Something or Other...but I can't seem to manage."

Martha glanced at the minister's face. She wasn't sure what she saw there. Concern? Pity? What if he thinks I'm mentally ill?

But it didn't matter anymore. The tiniest of breaches had been made in the dam that had held for a lifetime. It was about to burst. A little more help. Just a little more help. That's all she needed.

Reverend Thomas complied. "You are not alone, Martha. Sooner or later, everyone wrestles with doubt. Even I."

Reverend Thomas paused. When Martha lifted her head to look at him in surprise, he continued. "Oh, yes. Even I. Of course, I have learned to conquer my demons." He smiled. "Metaphorically speaking.

"Often, however, the way our parents reared us can have a rather direct bearing on when those doubts arise. And it goes without saying, the impact of our formative years can also gravely affect how we deal with those questions of faith — or it's absence.

"So, please...tell me — what was it like for you, growing up as a little girl?"

Martha twisted in her chair, in spite of herself remembering...remembering...vivid pictures of events long buried flashing spikes of painful, colored sadness.

"Martha," the minister said softly. "Don't be afraid to let it out. I assure you. You're safe here."

Safe. He had selected the right word. Martha stared at the topmost corner of the minister's desk blotter. Then she spoke.

"My parents..." she began. This was so scary. She had no idea what she was about to say. She opened her dry mouth and tried again.

"My parents...did not want me to believe...what other children believed." Martha felt as though she were picking her way through a mine field. "Before I was born, they made a decision not to subject me to the 'religious abuse' other children had to endure."

Martha looked up to see if she had offended Reverend Thomas. "Go on," he said. "It's all right."

"They felt it was their duty to 'demythologize' me," Martha continued. "Every time a religious holiday came around — Christmas, Easter, Thanksgiving — they would make a point of not celebrating it. The children at school would ask what I got for Christmas, or if I got a new dress for Easter — things like that."

"And what did you tell them?"

"At first, I made excuses, or changed the subject. Once or twice I lied and told them elaborate stories about what my parents had bought me."

Reverend Thomas slowly shook his head, a

sympathetic expression on his face.

"When I came home with questions, my parents were very understanding. They went to great lengths to explain to me why we didn't believe in God and why we couldn't participate in religious holidays. As I got older, they also encouraged me to stand up for my rights at school.

"So I did...but the results weren't very good. After a while, I became known as the class atheist. Some of them teased me, but mostly it wasn't like that...mostly it drove a wedge between me and the other children. I sometimes wondered if their parents warned them not to become friends with me..."

"That must have been difficult for you," said Reverend Thomas.

"Yes," said Martha. "It was very lonely."

"Is that when you began to resent your parents?"

"I don't resent my parents!" Martha said quickly. "They are wonderful people. They had every right to rear their child as they saw fit. Everything they did, they did for my own good. Except..."

"Except —?"

"Except...I think it was more than just my wanting to be like the other children. I think down deep I wanted to believe...if not in God, then in Something."

Reverend Thomas nodded. "I know exactly what you mean."

Martha could hardly believe that all of these words were coming from her lips. She had thought she would ask questions and let the minister do most of the talking. She had thought she needed answers.

But now she realized that many of the answers she already knew. What she needed most was to talk. And the longer she talked, the easier it became.

Much of it was due to Reverend Thomas. He knew just what to say, to keep her talking. He also knew when to sit quietly and listen. And she wasn't boring him. She could tell that he was intensely interested in everything she had to say, because he never took his eyes off her.

Martha's stomach still churned and her head hurt. Every so often she would shudder from a chill. But, oh, how good it felt to bare her soul!

As Martha continued to talk, she could feel the flood, the rush of dirty water that gushed forth from her innermost being. What sweet relief to learn that life — real life! — surged, boiled, spewed forth inside her.

She wasn't an empty room, after all. She wasn't hollow. Her fears were real. Her anger was real. Her needs were real.

She was real.

She talked. And talked. And talked. Bitter tears welled up in her eyes. Then her eyes spilled their acid contents down her cheeks, burning all the way down. She made no effort to wipe them away. She wanted to feel. Because what she felt was so, so good.

Martha barely noticed when the minister's secretary stuck her head in the door at 5:00. "Reverend, I'm getting ready to leave. Do you need anyth—"

Reverend Thomas cut her off with a wave of his hand. His piercing eyes never left Martha's face. The secretary retreated, softly closing the door behind her.

"Go on, Martha. You were saying —?"

And Martha continued. She told him everything he wanted to know — and he seemed to want to know everything. She talked about the embarrassing things that had happened to her and how those experiences had made her feel. Prompted by the minister's probing questions, she told him what she had thought, what she had said, what she had done. She told him things she thought she would never tell another living soul.

Eighty minutes later, the janitor tapped.
"Yes?"

"S'cuse me, Reverend," he apologized, just cracking the door. "Do you want I should lock up, or will you —"

"Yes. Lock up. I'm going to be awhile."

A short time later, Martha heard the muffled bang of the front door of the church, as the janitor departed.

And then the building was completely still.

Martha knew she was alone with Reverend Thomas, but she didn't care. This. This was all that mattered. She had never felt so sick. And she had never felt so close to getting well. Martha struggled to put her gratitude into words. "I...I can't tell you what this has meant to me. I don't usually —"

"I know."

There was a moment of silence.

"Well...I think I've said everything I need to say. I guess I had better be..." Martha felt lightheaded, dizzy. She pushed herself to her feet and tottered there, the backs of her calves pressing against the smooth, cool edge of the chair. She panted, as though she had just swam a storm-tossed, raging river, and now stood shivering, exhausted from the ordeal, on the opposite shore.

She could go now. She was going to be all right. That is, she would be, if she could somehow force her needley, nerve-numbed legs to walk.

Suddenly, Reverend Thomas stood up too, and banged his chair against the bookshelves behind.

"No! Not yet," he said, and quickly moved around the desk to stand in front of her.

That's strange, she thought. He was panting also.

"I —" he lifted his open palms above her trembling shoulders.

Another strange, she thought. He was also trembling.

"Don't — you shouldn't go...yet."

Confused, Martha looked into his flushed face. Was he sick, too?

"You need...you need to be seated," continued Reverend Thomas, his voice, somehow different, cracking. "We're...we're not finished. There's so much I need to —"

Martha jumped as she felt his warm hands come to rest on both her shoulders. He pushed gently, pushed her back down, down into her chair.

Martha stared straight ahead, her eyes focusing on the minister's silver belt buckle, six inches in front of her face.

His right hand left her shoulder and came to rest on his buckle. She watched his fingers work the black leather through the shiny metal opening. Martha blinked.

The minister's other hand smoothed its way along her shoulder toward the base of her neck. It turned and cupped her hair, then moved along the back of her scalp and gently drew her head forward.

Martha did not resist. She had no strength, no will to resist. She heard the crack of his stiff knees as he bent them double to crouch before her. Her eyes went out of focus as the minister pulled her face to his.

His face was rough against her tear-stained cheek. "Oh, Martha," the minister mumbled into her hair. "You have suffered so...you have suffered for so long."

He pulled back just a fraction. "Let me heal you, let me heal you on the inside, where you hurt."

His face angled slightly and came forward once again. Martha felt his mouth press against her dry lips. His sour tongue pushed between her slightly parted teeth and wriggled its way inside.

The minister's right hand arrived at her left breast at the same moment the odor of his Evel cologne reached her nostrils.

And Martha vomited the entire contents of her stomach directly into Reverend Thomas' open mouth.

THOUGH A MURDERER MIGHT!

WHY A MURDERER MIGHT

But Psyche, uplifting her finger,
Said: "Sadly this star I mistrust—
Her pallor I strangely mistrust"

—Edgar Allan Poe

1

Scott Miller pulled his jeep over on the right shoulder of the narrow, icy road, as far as he dared. This would have to do. He set the parking brake and turned off the ignition.

Outside it was utterly quiet — the kind of quiet that only heavy snow and high altitude isolation can bring. But inside his head the noise was deafening. Why was there a warrant for his arrest?

He had understood when they picked him up for questioning three weeks ago. After all, he was the ex-husband of the woman who had the most to gain from figure-skater Kelly Astin's murder.

Again and again, the networks had shown the

grainy video in agonizing slow motion, taken by a fan at Kelly's last practice. Attired in satin blue, she had just completed her Olympic routine, arms extended heavenward. She even rehearsed her trademark winner's smile.

Suddenly, the dark, neat dot appeared an inch above the bridge of her nose, snapping her head straight back and changing the look on her face to one of mild surprise. As the camera lens jerkily zoomed in, Kelly's expression didn't change. Not when her legs crumpled underneath her. Not as she slumped backward in a limp heap, arms spread wide. Not even as the exit wound in the back of her head began to darken her brown hair in a red pool of blood on the ice.

Scott shook his head in a futile attempt to clear the stark image from his mind.

Late last night there had been a break in the investigation. A marksman named Billy Maxwell, who had been fired from a S.W.A.T. team one month earlier, had been taken into custody. Found in his possession was a rifle matching the caliber of the weapon that had killed Kelly Astin.

And now this morning, apparently as a result of an all-night interrogation of Maxwell, it was everywhere on the news: Scott Miller was wanted for murder!

Scott had never heard of Billy Maxwell. But he was beginning to wonder if he knew someone who had.

It was time to go see.

2

Scott got out of the jeep and carefully pushed the door shut with a quiet click. He didn't want her to hear or see anything that might tip her off that he was coming.

He checked the hastily scrawled map and then began to climb the steep embankment. He would soon find out if their mutual friend Jim Schwartz, who lived in Eugene, Oregon, had leveled with him about the location of his wife's hideaway cabin.

Scott had been married to the feisty figure-skater Janet Taylor for exactly 19 months and 11 days. Although seven years older than the 23-year-old phenom, he had fallen for Janet like a high school freshman with an uncontrollable crush the very first time he laid eyes on her.

That was only two years ago. Surfing through channels in his Dallas apartment on a slow TV night, he was already two stations past ESPN when he sat bolt upright. A prickling sensation swept up his spine. He had just seen the face of the woman he had been searching for all his life.

Click-click. There.

Oh, dear God. She was gorgeous! She was a floating, twirling, dream-on-skates come true. She was the vision of all he had ever longed to make his own. She was...gone!

Abruptly, the picture had switched to NBA highlights of the Bulls-Knicks game. No! He didn't want basketball. He wanted her.

But who was she? Panic overtook him. He could not — would not! — lose her now. Scott picked up the phone, got ESPN's number from the long-distance operator, phoned the network and demanded to know the name of the figure-skater who had been on his screen two minutes ago.

Nobody knew.

He pushed. Insisted. Demanded.

Would not take "No," for an answer.

After bumping him from person to person and keeping him on hold forever, finally they connected him directly with the show's producer, who identified her: Janet Taylor, best female figure skater in the world.

3

Scott paused midway up the mountain to lean against a scrawny pine and catch his breath. He had never been much of an athlete. Funny. What he had always heard must be true: opposites attract.

He and Janet were radically different. She liked to party — he preferred quiet evenings at home. She was a hawkish gun enthusiast who loved to blow things away on the target range — he was a pacifist who donated money to any politician who favored gun control.

She was addicted to TV — he almost never found anything on the tube worth watching, so he read — books, magazines, newspapers. The only thing she read was her daily horoscope.

They did have one thing in common, however: they were both passionate, driven people. She was obsessed with winning an Olympic gold medal. He was obsessed with her.

Scott had given the ESPN producer no rest until the poor man promised to send him a video tape of the raw footage their cameraman had taken of Janet's last competition. The day the package from ESPN arrived, Scott walked straight from the mailbox to his VCR, inserted the tape with trembling fingers, turned on his television and...there she was — more beautiful, more graceful, more desirable than any woman had a right to be.

Scott forgot to eat supper. He sat in the dark and played the tape over and over and over again. Frustrated by the brevity of the clip, he suddenly remembered that his VCR could play it back in slow

motion.
Much better.
Freeze frame was better still.
Finally, muscles in his back screaming, eyes burning, Scott glanced at his watch. It couldn't be 2:55 a.m.
No matter. He knew what he had to do.
Next morning, Scott called the plant and quit his job. Then he called his best friend, Jeff Forster, and agreed to sell Jeff his beloved '57 Mustang for the price Scott had laughed at two weeks ago.
He hung up the phone and glanced around the small apartment that had been home for six years and started packing. He would forfeit two months' rent and his deposit, he knew, but he had a plane to catch.
To Portland, Oregon.
To the place where she lived and trained.
To the woman whose haunting face and lithe form had burned a hole in his soul.
His plane touched down at the Portland Airport the next morning at 11:53. The other passengers shuffled down to baggage claim. Scott strode to the nearest bank of pay phones.
The Portland Oregonian sports reporter who answered the phone had no idea where ice skater Janet Taylor trained. But the sports columnist he checked with did. Now Scott knew on which side of town to start looking for an apartment.

4

There! At the top of the rise to his left, nearly hidden by the trees, was the cabin, just as Jim had said. Lightheaded and winded, Scott designated one of his gasps for air as a sigh of relief.
Now. All he had to do was somehow negotiate the last two hundred feet to her cabin before she saw him

and had a chance to hop into her car and speed away. He must approach unseen and unheard.

Right. After the exhausting climb, Scott had no strength left to dart from tree to tree in the snow. Better rest here for a moment, he decided.

Scott looked around until he found a fallen tree eighteen feet to his right where he could hunker down and hide. Once there, he sank to his knees, panting. A moment later, he gave in to his aching muscles and eased his body down until he was lying flat on his back in the snow.

He was much warmer here, as though the powdery snow were some kind of thermal blanket. Scott let his eyelids close. He wouldn't lie here long, he told himself. Just for a second.

And while he lay there his mind drifted...

Scott warmed with the memory of that electric moment when Janet first realized he existed. He smiled for the first time in a long while.

Twenty minutes into her 6:00 a.m. training regimen, Janet had suddenly broken away and skated directly toward Scott, who leaned over the plexiglass barrier at the north end of the rink. She came to a sudden stop three feet away from him, her skates cutting hard, shushing out a fine, white spray of ice.

"Who are you?" she demanded.

"My name is Scott Mitchell."

"What are you doing here?"

"Watching you."

"I can see that. For the past three mornings —

"Four." Scott smiled.

"All right — for the past four mornings, from the time I've stepped on the ice till the time I've left, you haven't taken your eyes off me."

"That's right."

"Are you a skater?" she asked, eyes narrowing.

"Not even close."

"What are you, then, a fan?"

"I'm a lot more than that, Janet," said Scott.

Janet cocked one elbow, fist against muscular hip, and sighed, rolling her eyes. "Look. You're bugging me, all right? Breaking my concentration. I come here to train — so give me a break. Just go."

Shaking her head exasperatedly, she turned and skated away. Her blonde pony tail whipped back and forth behind her.

Scott stayed.

Ten minutes later she skated up again.

"I thought I told you to leave."

"I'm sorry," said Scott. "I can't."

"Do you want me to call security?" Janet threatened.

"You don't need to do that," said Scott, softly. "I'm not going to hurt you."

"Tell it to security." She skated toward the rink office.

"Wait!" called Scott. "Don't go."

She paused, hands on hips, her back to Scott...but listening.

"Janet," Scott pleaded. He gripped the plexiglass and leaned out over the barrier. His voice broke. "I quit my job, sold my car and flew halfway across the country just to get to know you. Does that sound like someone who wants to hurt you?"

She hesitated another five seconds without turning around. Then she skated away. But she did not go to the rink office.

Scott's heart pounded in his ears. He doggedly clung to his post and watched, as Janet completed her morning routine. Was it his imagination, Scott wondered, or had the second half of her workout been much crisper? He thought that her footwork was quicker than he had seen it, her jumps higher.

As usual, Janet skated to a stop in front of her navy blue equipment bag and lifted out a small white towel.

But this time she pushed off and glided toward the north end of the rink, while she blotted the perspiration from her neck and face.

She stopped directly in front of Scott. She draped the towel around the back of her neck and locked eyes with his steady gaze.

"Why?" she asked.

5

Scott knew he should get up and make his move toward the cabin before it got dark. But he didn't want to open his eyes. Not yet.

That single-word question had been the beginning of a daring new world for both of them. Janet got a full taste of the thick, clinging honey of pure devotion. Scott got to revel in the wonder of finally discovering someone he loved more than himself.

To prove the depth of his love, Scott stormed her, swarmed her, surrounded her. Everything he said and did fed her bottomless need for attention and constant praise. Taking it as her due, Janet drew what she needed from the vial of his heart and injected it like a drug.

For her, marriage to Scott was a way to stay high. Scott's round-the-clock devotion enabled her to endure the daily pain and mindless monotony of training. It helped her pursue the only thing that really mattered — Olympic gold.

6

The grin began to fade from Scott's face as he lay in the snow. He shivered with a cold he felt all the way to his bones. Scott rubbed his eyes and stiffly pushed himself up to one elbow. Blinking, he tried to find the outline of the cabin through the trees. But he still wasn't ready to go.

Six months after their wedding Scott's love for Janet was stronger than ever. But it was no longer blind. He had begun to come to grips with the fact that his wife was incapable of loving him in return.

Her ability to love him would remain blocked, Scott became convinced, until she had climbed in triumph to the top level of that Olympic platform and bowed her head to receive golden, glimmering proof that she was the best in the world.

7

The light was starting to fade. Scott had wasted precious time.

Steeling himself, Scott peered over the fallen tree and mapped out a circuitous approach to the cabin that would afford him maximum cover. He looked left, right, behind him, to make sure it was clear. Nothing.

He closed his eyes once more and took a deep breath. He rose to a painful crouch and, staying as low as possible, pushed off toward a crooked evergreen fifteen feet ahead.

Scott was so cold he could hardly move. But as he stumbled across the uneven ground from one tree to the next, the cold he felt inside was even worse.

Kelly Astin's meteoric rise to the top of the figure skating world cost him his marriage.

Less than a year after their wedding, Janet began losing to Kelly in head-to-head competition. Everybody else credited Kelly's new coach.

Janet blamed Scott. All she knew was that before she met him, she was number one in the world. Now she was number two. To her, it was a no-brainer. Scott had to go.

Their last five months together were frozen hell.

First, Janet stopped having sex with Scott. "Just keep your cottin'-pickin' hands off of me," she told him. "You're sapping me of energy I need out on the ice!"

Then she shut him out of her bedroom altogether. "How do you expect me to get the rest I need, with your tossing and turning all night?"

The constant attention she once craved was now smothering to her. She didn't want Scott to hold her, to stroke her hair — not even to massage her practice-weary feet and calves, as he used to do every night. His very presence was an insufferable irritation, the way he hovered near, looking at her. Always looking at her.

"Give me some space — get out and make some friends," she told him. "Get out and find a hobby," she said. "Get out and go for a drive, for crying out loud!" It became increasingly clear, she wanted him to just get out.

Even so, the sheaf of divorce papers in the sheriff's hand had been a shock. Next day at work Scott was served with a restraining order which prevented him from returning to her apartment to attempt to reason with her. Her phone had been changed to a private number.

Last month, the divorce became final. As suddenly as Scott had entered her life, he had now been kicked out of it. With no contact, no word, Scott sometimes awakened in the night seized by an eerie sensation that the past two years had been nothing more than a dream...until Kelly Astin slumped to the ice.

Suddenly, everyone remembered who Scott Miller had been married to. The media descended on

Portland and combed the city for clues, quotes, confessions, denials. When the more aggressive reporters tired of Janet's stubborn silence and Scott's stammering bewilderment, they reported rumors and printed lies.

Scott watched every newscast he could find, taping some that aired simultaneously, programming his VCR to capture others while he was at work. It was his only chance to catch a glimpse of Janet, to uncover a tidbit here, another there, about what she was up to...even if not all of it was true. It sent a ripple of pleasure up his spine every time a reporter mistakenly referred to him as Janet's husband, rather than her ex. As far as Scott was concerned, the reporter had made no mistake.

Finally, things slowed down. Until three days ago, a stubborn contingent still set up cameras at the practice rink each day and reported on Janet's every spill as "proof that the pressure was starting to tell." But when Janet dropped out of sight, most of them shrugged their shoulders and lost interest. Once again, Scott had been able to drive to work without being followed.

But this morning's stunning development made him headline news. Back in the city below, Scott knew that scores of reporters, unleashed by word of the warrant for his arrest, were even now crawling all over the plant where he worked, cruising the streets he usually drove, staking out his apartment, picking through his garbage.

He had to hurry. It was only a matter of time before they —

"Crack!"

Scott heard the report of the rifle a split-second before the slug slammed into his chest and knocked him to the ground.

The sound of running feet closed rapidly. "You

fool!"

Scott recognized the wildcat scream.

Janet.

8

Scott tried to rise. But as soon as he lifted his head, all of his remaining strength drained out of him. His head flopped back on the snow. His fingers twitched and the muscles in his legs jerked spasmodically. Scott lay staring up at the sky.

Suddenly, Janet stood over him, rifle in her right hand, blocking the light. Her face was contorted with anger. She screamed again. "You fool! Why did you come here? Who told you where I was?" She jammed the butt of the rifle against her shoulder and pointed its barrel at Scott's face. "Who?"

He was in shock, but Scott wasn't afraid. "Janet." Scott paused to swallow. "There's a warrant for —"

"—your arrest. I know. I said, 'Who told you where —' wait a minute. It was Jim, wasn't it? Wasn't it?"

Scott did not reply.

"Quit looking at me like that!"

"It's...it's been so long since..." Scott coughed. Fluid was filling his right lung.

"Yeah, well, it's going to be a lot longer where you're going," said Janet. "When I saw you trying to sneak up on the cabin, I called the police. They'll be here any minute."

"Janet, I swear!" said Scott, once again trying to lift his head. "I don't know Billy Maxwell. I never heard his name before today."

"No kidding," said Janet.

Scott coughed again. He felt pain now. "You...you know that I don't —?"

"You are such a fool." She shook her head.

"Janet...why did you call the police?" asked Scott. He was beginning to have trouble keeping his thoughts straight. "You know I would never...in a thousand years...hurt you..."
"That's not what the police think."
He could barely hear her. His eyes drooped shut.
"They think you came up here after calling me and threatening, 'If I can't have you, nobody will.' "

9

TIME Magazine made Scott's trial its cover story. A photo of the rifle used to shoot Kelly Astin divided the cover diagonally. The picture in the upper left-hand corner showed a smiling Janet, moments after landing a triple in the compulsaries at the last Olympics. In the lower right-hand corner was the now-famous newswire photo of Kelly Astin's body, blood pooling on the ice beneath her head moments after she was shot. Inset beneath the picture of his ex-wife was a two-inch square photograph of Scott being led away in handcuffs after the trial.

The story began on page fifty-four, under a headline in two-inch high red letters that said, "NOW WE KNOW!":

> In what seasoned observers were calling the shortest murder trial in recent memory, a jury of nine men and three women last week found Scott Miller guilty of conspiracy to commit murder, in the shooting death of figure skater Kelly Astin.
>
> The defendant's ex-wife, Olympic gold medalist Janet Taylor, was the state's star witness. Taylor testified she divorced Miller because of his repeated threats to murder Astin. Taylor said Miller "became fixated on the ridiculous notion" that Astin had to

be "eliminated" in order to preserve the financial bonanza Miller expected to reap when his wife won Olympic gold.

Just as damaging was a typewritten facsimile letter the prosecution entered into evidence. The fax hired gunman Billy Maxwell to "take out Kelly Astin as a surprise early birthday present for my wife." Two handwriting experts confirmed that the signature at the bottom of the fax was Miller's. Phone company records indicated the fax was sent from an all-night convenience store two blocks from the Portland apartment Miller had rented after being evicted by his ex-wife.

The jury's unanimous recommendation for the death penalty came as something of a shock. However, one of the jurors, who asked not to be identified, told TIME, "As far as we were concerned, [Miller's] refusal to take the stand and testify [in his own defense] amounted to a confession of guilt."

Rumors persist that Miller refused to cooperate with his state-appointed defense attorney, James Fallon. A source close to Fallon's office claimed that Miller had not spoken "three words to anyone" throughout the trial.

When asked how soon sentence might be carried out, Chief Prosecutor Melvin Berkowitz said, "That depends. Normally, the appeal process drags on for years." Citing Miller's "apparent disinterest," however, Berkowitz speculated that if Miller refused to initiate any appeals of his own, execution could take place "as soon as eighteen months."

10

Seven hours before Scott was scheduled to die by lethal injection, a guard unlocked the door to his solitary cell.

"Let's go, Miller!" he barked. "You got a visitor."

Slumped on the edge of his iron cot, Scott didn't look up. "I don't want to see anybody."

"Suit yourself," said the guard and turned to leave. "If it was me, I wouldn't want to see her either."

"Her?" Scott was on his feet. "What do you mean, her?"

"Your ex-wife."

"Janet?" cried Scott, rushing to the door. "Janet's here? Yes! Yes, I want to see her! Take me to her, please!"

11

Handcuffed, a guard on either arm, Scott was led out of his cell. A few hours from now they would make him stumble down the short hall to his left. But on this trip, they steered him into the longer hall to his right, which led to maximum security visitation.

The harshly-lit room was bare, save for the long, narrow table that butted up against the wall of bullet-proof glass. No one else was in the room.

His guards took him to the far-left cubicle and strapped his ankles onto the legs of a cold metal chair that was anchored to the floor. Next they short-chained his cuffed wrists to the metal ring that protruded from the top of the table. One of them walked over to a chair in the opposite corner of the room, leaned back and read a magazine while the other went to get his visitor.

Scott waited, with nothing to do but stare at the

thick, discolored glass. He wondered if Janet had changed her mind. Then a sliding metal door creaked on its rollers and banged to a stop.

And she was there.

12

"Here he is," said the guard. "I'll be back to get you in ten minutes."

"Ten — wait!" Scott yelled after him. "We need more time!"

But the guard, deaf to inmate complaints, was already at the door. A moment later it banged shut.

Scott had written her repeatedly, begging to see her one last time. She didn't reply. But though he had long ago given up hope that this meeting would occur, he had pictured how it would be, in intimate detail, a thousand times.

Now that it was here, it was almost over.

When she sat down, Scott automatically reached out toward her, but the short chain kept his manacled hands from touching the glass. He had pictured it all wrong. He couldn't hold her in his arms, couldn't feel her breath warm against his cheek, couldn't tenderly kiss her good-bye.

At first she wouldn't make direct eye contact, so he said nothing and waited.

Scott was shocked by her appearance. Her eyes had dark, puffy circles under them. Her skin color was bad, though he didn't know how much of it was due to the corridor light. Had she been ill? She looked ten hard years older.

Still she wouldn't look at him. Nine minutes left, and their first minute had been spent in silence.

Scott could bear it no longer. Bending forward with his lips near the vent, he looked up at her. "Janet?"

At the faint sound of her name, she instinctively looked down and their eyes met. Scott fought back the tears. "Thank you for coming," he said.

He saw her lips move, but couldn't quite make out what she had said. When he shook his head, Janet rolled her eyes and reluctantly bent down to the brass vent. Now their eyes were level with each other, barely eight inches apart.

"I said, I didn't come here for your thanks."

Her tone hurt. But Scott nodded, to keep her down there, talking.

Eight minutes to go.

"At least you've come."

Janet's voice remained hard. "Only to ask you a question."

"All right," said Scott slowly. And he waited.

Janet's eyes bored into his. "Why?"

Scott catapulted back in time, remembering that she had asked that same question the first day they met. She didn't understand him then. And now, on their last day, she still could not comprehend the depth of his love for her.

"You don't know?" Scott said. His voice broke.

"How could I?" snapped Janet. "How could anybody figure out someone like you?"

"All through the trial," Scott said, "every day I've spent in here, waiting — my one consolation was that somehow you knew...that finally, you understood..."

"Understood what?" Janet yelled.

Scott waited a long time before replying. When he spoke, his voice was barely loud enough for her to hear. "Understood how much I love you," he said.

Seven minutes to go.

"Don't start with that," said Janet. "Look..." The hard edge came off her voice only slightly. "It wasn't supposed to happen this way."

"Then why did you lie about me on the stand?"

"Because I had no choice. You know that."

"And the fax with my signature on it?"

"You never did like to pay attention to all the stuff you had to sign, did you, Scott?"

"I figured the fax must have been somewhere in the middle of those things you gave me to sign the night before the sheriff served me with divorce papers."

"Is that what you thought?"

"But if so...if you're the one who tricked me into signing that fax...that means you're the one who hired Billy Maxwell to murder Kelly."

Janet shrugged. "Why would I do that? I would have beaten her in the Olympics, anyway."

"I believed that," agreed Scott. He hesitated, then said what they both knew was true. "But you didn't."

Janet looked away.

Six minutes to go.

"You were supposed to hire one of those famous defense lawyers," blurted Janet. Her restless gaze fixed on his handcuffs. "God knows there were enough of them, salivating over the worldwide publicity they'd get. All you had to do was go with anybody but that moron they assigned you. Any lawyer in the world but him."

"I was afraid to," said Scott.

"What was there to be afraid of?" she cried, facing him again. "If you would have just cooperated, any of them could have gotten you off for...for temporary insanity...for grief over the divorce — any number of things. The jury would've bought it."

Janet shook her head exasperatedly. "All you had to do was take the stand in your own defense! That sincere puppy dog look of yours would have made them feel sorry for you. Not one of those women would have voted for the death penalty. With your clean record, the most they would've given you was ten...fifteen years — with half off for good behavior. She looked down. "I was going to make it up to you..."

"How?" asked Scott.

Five minutes.

"With the money," said Janet.

Scott flinched. "The endorsement money?"

"That's right," she said defensively. "With all the publicity from the trial, there was more than I thought there would be. You could have lived in luxury. You would never have had to punch a time clock again."

Unbelievable, thought Scott. Unbelievable. He sank back in his chair and stared at the wall.

Janet bore the silence as long as she could. "Well. If you don't want to talk any more, I guess I'd...better..."

"No!" said Scott. He lunged forward. "Don't...don't leave me." His body shook. "There's so much we have to...to say to each other. There's so much..." Scott pressed his forehead against his tightly-clenched fists. He had to get control of himself. There was something he desperately had to ask.

He raised his head, eyes searching her face. Softly: "How did it feel, winning the gold medal?"

Scott thought she hadn't heard. But her expression gave her away. She had heard. Her answer was important to Scott. Extremely important. So he waited.

"It was..." Janet began, then stopped herself. "It was the worst moment of my life."

"Don't say that." Scott's reaction was immediate.

"You're the only one I've told that to," said Janet quietly.

"But why? You threw away your childhood, gave up your social life, spent eighteen years of your life working for that one moment. You sacrificed everything — even me!"

Janet's eyes seemed focused on something far away. "Yeah. That's what ruined it for me. I stepped up on the platform, and someone stuck some wilted flowers in my hand. Then after they hung that cheap medal around my neck, I remember thinking, 'This is it? This is what I've given up everything in my life to achieve?'

Four.

"It wasn't enough. That's what kept going through my head over and over again, while that stupid band butchered 'The Star Spangled Banner': 'This isn't enough.' And then it was over and I had to step down so someone else could climb up and pretend that it was the greatest thing that had ever happened to them."

Janet's chin quivered. "Everybody kept asking, 'How does it feel? How does it feel?' At first I told them, 'I don't think it's sunk in, yet.'

"But they wouldn't let it rest. They kept pushing and pushing to get me to say what they wanted to hear. So finally I said it: 'It was the greatest moment of my life.' And then they shut up and left me alone."

Janet wiped at her eyes with her fingers, leaving runny black streaks on both cheeks.

"I'm sorry," said Scott. "I wanted that medal almost as much as you did. When you won, I was so proud, so happy for you." Scott paused. "I want you to know something else, too. You were right — it wouldn't have made any difference if Kelly had been there. Nobody could have beaten you that night."

"Right," said Janet sarcastically. "I just wish I —" She closed her mouth.

Three.

This wasn't going as he had hoped. But their time was almost gone. He had to press on, to get it all out. Scott looked down. "I...I didn't tell you everything. Somehow I thought that after you'd won..." He couldn't finish.

"What?" asked Janet impatiently.

Scott took a big breath. "That...that you'd

be...grateful. That you'd want to come back to me and try again, just the two of us. At least until..."

"Grateful?" howled Janet. "Whatever for? I had to ditch you to get my life back together. You almost cost me the gold!"

"I thought you'd be grateful..." Scott could barely say it. "Grateful for not...turning you in."

"Oh, get real," said Janet. "And what did you have on me? Nothing! What were you going to do — tell them I hid the fax in the papers you signed? I would have denied it! You had no proof, Scott."

Two.

Scott stared at the brass vent. "You know the night Billy Maxwell got the fax?"

"What about it?"

"I wasn't in Portland," said Scott. "I couldn't have sent it."

Janet thought a moment. "So — where were you?"

"As soon as I got off work, I drove down to Eugene. I was feeling pretty low, that day. Decided I'd drop in on Jim Schwartz."

"No way," said Janet. "I know Jim. He would have come forward at the trial, if you had been with him that night."

"Yeah, well, I wasn't," admitted Scott. "I went to his house and rang the doorbell a couple of times, but he wasn't home."

"He's always home."

"That's why I didn't bother to call first. Anyway, by the time I gave up on him, it was late. I was almost out of gas, so I stopped and filled up the tank before I drove back."

"As usual, you paid cash," said Janet.

"Yes, but I hadn't eaten anything since lunch, and I was hungry. So I decided to get a burger."

"And then you drove back to Portland?" Janet interrupted. "That's it? That's your story? Who saw you? Who knew you well enough to recognize you?"

"Nobody."

One.

"Scott, without witnesses the jury wouldn't have —"

"In a way, I did have a witness."

"You just said —"

"You know those automatic teller machines?" asked Scott, "—the ones that give you cash after banking hours."

"What about them?"

"Well, it took more money than I figured to fill up the tank. All I had left was a dollar and change — not enough to buy a burger and fries and —"

"Are you trying to tell me you used your card to get some money from the machine?" asked Janet.

"Yes," said Scott.

"And you think that proves you were in Eugene? Scott, anybody could have used your card to get money."

"Not without my P.I.N., they couldn't."

"They could have, if you gave it to them. Don't you see, Scott? The prosecutor would have just used that against you, to prove you were trying to set up an alibi. Everybody knows you and Jim Schwartz were friends. He could have done it."

"Jim Schwartz was your friend, too, Janet. He would never have helped me at your expense."

"You mean like he did when he told you how to find my cabin?" said Janet. "Sorry, Scott. It wouldn't have worked."

"I guess this ATM was in a high crime area, or something," continued Scott.

"Scott, please," said Janet. "Give it up. There's no way you could have proved beyond a shadow of a doubt that you were in —"

"There was this sign right above the window." Scott bit his lip. "It said something like: 'For our customers' protection, a photographic record is kept of

each person making a transaction.' "
Janet's face froze.
"I checked," said Scott. "It's this bank's policy to keep all ATM records for five years." He paused. He desperately needed it to sink in. "Darling...my picture has been there all this time."
Janet gasped and stood up, knocking her chair backward. The clatter echoed in the empty hall.
"Janet, Honey..." cried Scott, straining to be heard through the vent. "I didn't mean to frighten you — I only wanted you to know you didn't take my life from me...I gave it!"
"No!" Janet cried. "No!" She clapped one hand to her mouth. Her shoulders heaved. Sobs wracked her body. Her knees buckled.
Neither of them noticed the hallway door had rolled opened until the guard stood beside her. "Ma'am?" he said, eyeing her warily. "It's time."
Janet wheeled on the guard and balled her fists. "You stay away from me!" she screamed.
Turning, she fell to her knees in front of Scott, mouth against the vent. "Why?" she wailed. "Why? I don't understand how you...how you could —"
"Say it," said Scott.
Seeing the commotion, the second guard threw down his magazine, exited Scott's room and quickly ran toward them.
"Janet!" called Scott. "Say it! God, please — say it!"
Both guards arrived at either side of her now. They pulled her away.
"Say it!" cried Scott.
Nearly to the doorway, Janet flexed her powerful legs and twisted free from one guard. Still sobbing, she faced Scott for a last, brief instant. Bent nearly double, she shouted something. Then the angry guard recovered, grabbed her left arm — and she was gone.
Scott couldn't hear her words. But he read her

lips. Finally, she had said it:
"I don't understand how you could love me this much!"

13

Scott slowly leaned back in his chair and closed his eyes. They would be in to get him any minute. But for now, he was alone.

His pulse quickened. His breath deepened.

He saw himself step up to the top platform and bow his head to receive the medal. It gleamed, golden and pure, in the sunlight.

The band struck up a rousing rendition of "The Star Spangled Banner." Scott saw himself raise both hands skyward in triumph. He smiled. He waved.

Well-wishers crowded around. The media stuck microphones in front of his face. "How does it feel?" they all wanted to know.

Scott told them the truth:

"This is the greatest moment of my life."

THOUGH A MURDERER MIGHT!

THE DAY OF YOUR LIFE

All these — all the meanness
  and agony without end
I sitting look out upon,
See, hear, and am silent.

—Walt Whitman

Now do you understand why you won't go to heaven?

If not, don't force it.
  It may not come when you expect it.
  It may not come where you expect it.
  It may not come the way you expect it.
  It may not come through whom you expect it.

All roads do not lead to heaven anymore than all keys fit the lock on your front door. But one of the keys out there does.

If you are meant to understand — and if you keep looking — one day that key will show up in your pocket. You may even find that it has been there all along.

One thing more.

Understanding is not enough.

Suppose a man placed the cold barrel of a loaded pistol against your right temple. Suppose you heard him cock the hammer. Suppose, out of the corner of your eye, you watched his finger begin to squeeze the trigger.

You may understand that the moment the hammer comes forward, the firing pin will strike and ignite the primer, which will, in turn, ignite the gunpowder, creating a miniature explosion inside the shell that will hurl the bullet at high velocity down the length of the barrel.

You may understand that upon impact with your skull, the bullet will flatten slightly on one side, widening its striking surface and altering its path as it tears through your cerebrum and exits on the other side, carrying with it bits of ear, bone, blood and brain.

So long as you stand there and do nothing, however, your understanding will not save your life.

MARRIAGE INTERNATIONAL PRESENTS —

The

Trilogy

For everyone who is married:

- *Who is about to give up and get a divorce...*

- *Or whose relationship is stable but mediocre...*

- *Or who has a great marriage but wants to see how much higher it can soar –*

MARRIAGES CAN BE SAVED!

TOUGH TALK
TO A STUBBORN SPOUSE

by **STEPHEN**

- *The bestselling book that is saving hopeless marriages nationwide.*

- *As seen on* Oprah, Sally Jesse Raphael, *and scores of talk shows around the country.*

- *Sixty-one short, blistering chapters that speak the language of the spouse who has decided to call it quits!* →

ISBN: 0-89081-783-9   286 Pages

Why Did I Say "I Do?"

Remembering The Dream and Making It Happen

by **STEPHEN**

Part I
   Start by assessing the State of Your Union and take the most thorough self-evaluation test of your marriage available today.

Part II
   Understand why it is so hard to build a great marriage.

Part III
   This section will rock you to your core – Discover a whole new set of reasons to stay married! →

ISBN: 0-89081-987-4   340 Pages

FOR LOVERS ONLY

The Truly Intimate Marriage

BY STEPHEN & JUDITH

FOR RISK-TAKING COUPLES ONLY!

· *Stephen and his wife Judith take you to the heart of marital communication with a single secret that will help remove the destructive, critical attitudes from your relationship.*

· *Then they launch you on an eye-opening, heart-thumping, lovemaking journey through the stars!* →

ISBN: 0-89081-865-7   248 Pages

TOUGH TALK
TO A STUBBORN SPOUSE
•$8.95 plus $1.50 postage and handling

Why Did I Say "I Do?"
•$8.95 plus $1.50 postage and handling

FOR LOVERS ONLY
•$7.95 plus $1.50 postage and handling

Or...

Own the entire
Trilogy
of three marriage-transforming books for just $24.95, postage & handling included!

Please use the blanks to indicate how many of each item you are ordering. Add $1.50 postage/handling for each book – or none for The Trilogy. (Indiana residents only: add 5% sales tax.)

- **TOUGH TALK TO A STUBBORN SPOUSE**
  _____copy(ies) at $8.95 = _____

- **WHY DID I SAY "I DO?"**
  _____copy(ies) at $8.95 = _____

- **FOR LOVERS ONLY**
  _____copy(ies) at $7.95 = _____

- **THE TRILOGY (all three books)**
  _____set(s) at $24.95 = _____

Total books:	$_____
Total postage & handling:	$_____
(Indiana residents only) 5% Sales Tax:	$_____
Total Amount Enclosed:	$_____

OR CALL 1-800-496-6846 AND ORDER TOLL-FREE!

Name_____

Address_____

City_____State_____Zip_____

Please enclose check or money order payable to:
100th Century Publishing
5110 Lincoln Avenue•Evansville, IN 47715

Please charge to my Visa/Mastercard #_____

Expiration Date_____Signature_____